THE LIGHT
OF COMMON DAY

Realism in American Fiction

THE LIGHT
OF COMMON DAY

Realism in American Fiction

EDWIN H. CADY

INDIANA UNIVERSITY PRESS

Bloomington / London

To Benjamin Townley Spencer

*from whom I first heard of "realism" and,
indeed, of American literature*

*The best light on a statue is the light of the
common marketplace.*

—MICHELANGELO

*. . . trailing clouds of glory do we come
From God: who is our home. . . .
At length the Man perceives it die away,
And fade into the light of common day.*

—WORDSWORTH

*The life of man is the true romance. . . .
and that is ever the difference between the
wise and the unwise: the latter wonders at
what is unusual; the wise man wonders at the usual.*

—EMERSON

*The mysteries of human nature surpass the
'mysteries of redemption,' for the infinite we
only suppose, while we see the finite.*

—EMILY DICKINSON

*. . . an American novel, . . . keeping in the light of
common day an action whose springs are in the
darkest fastnesses of the human soul.*

—HOWELLS

C O N T E N T S

PREFACE

THOUGH IDEALLY THE AUTHOR MIGHT PREFER TO LET HIS
themes grow upon the reader's imagination without
generalizing intervention, perhaps it is advisable at least
to name the intentions of *The Light of Common Day*. The
book attempts: (1) to render "realism" and associated
terms more applicable and serviceable to literary discussion; (2) to clarify a view of that portion of American
literary history usually called the movement or period of
realism; (3) in using and illustrating the ideas and view-
points necessary to (1) and (2) to propose some ap-
proaches to and conclusions in literary criticism; and (4)
to observe certain consequences for the serious teaching
of literature which seem to follow.

It is therefore a book of interconnected essays, literary but personal, expressions more of experience and
conviction than of scholarship. The aim is to record what
happens when one shifts his point of view, to see how
things look from another angle of vision, in a different
light. The author is aware that there are other lights. His
is a minority view, and he gladly acknowledges fundamental debts to the insights of the majority. His plea is
that of Stephen Crane: "I understand that a man is born

into the world with his own pair of eyes, and he is not at all responsible for his vision—he is merely responsible for his quality of personal honesty. . . . I, however, do not say that I am honest—I merely say that I am as nearly honest as a weak mental machinery will allow."

ACKNOWLEDGMENTS

CHAPTERS 6 AND 7 AND PORTIONS OF CHAPTER 10 HAVE BEEN published before. I am grateful to the Ohio State University Press for permission to reprint " 'The Wizard Hand,' Hawthorne, 1864–1900," which appeared in longer form in Roy Harvey Pearce, ed., *Hawthorne Centenary Essays,* 1964; to *The Mad River Review* for permission to reprint "The Howells Nobody Knows" from Vol. I, no. 1, Winter, 1964–65; and to the National Council of Teachers of English for permission to reprint excerpts from "The Teacher and the American Novel: 1964," in Lewis Leary, ed., *The Teacher and American Literature,* 1965.

Student audiences have been kind to portions of this book read to them at Duke, Indiana, Richmond, St. Lawrence, and Syracuse Universities, Oberlin College, and the Universities of Cincinnati, Notre Dame, and Miami, Ohio. Among my Indiana University students who have been especially helpful are John Crowley, Richard Curtis, Henry Sparapani, and Thomas Wortham. Carolyn Wolfcale worked patiently at successive manuscripts.

For professional insights generously offered I cordially thank my colleagues Don Cook, Philip Daghlian, James Justus, Terence Martin, and Wallace Williams.

ACKNOWLEDGMENTS

They encouraged me mightily, as did Joe Lee Davis; but none of them is to blame for any of my solecisms.

Finally, there are the thanks I incessantly owe to my wife, Norma W. Cady, for many things new and old. The book might properly have been dedicated to her except that she joins happily in the actual dedication's salute of deep affection from us both.

E. H. C.

Bloomington, 1971

THE LIGHT
OF COMMON DAY

Realism in American Fiction

1 / "Realism":

Toward a Definition

THE FACE OF THE WATER, *in time, became a wonderful book—a book that was a dead language to the uneducated passenger, but which told its mind to me without reserve, delivering its most cherished secrets as clearly as if it uttered them with a voice. . . . There never was so wonderful a book written by man; never one whose interest was so absorbing, so unflagging, so sparklingly renewed with every re-perusal. . . . In truth, the passenger who could not read this book saw nothing but all manner of pretty pictures in it, painted by the sun and shaded by the clouds, whereas to the trained eye these were not pictures at all, but the grimmest and most dead-earnest of reading-matter.*

Now when I had mastered the language of this water, and had come to know every trifling feature that bordered the great river as familiarly as I knew the letters of the alphabet, I had made a valuable acquisition. But I had lost something, too. I had lost something which could never be restored to me while I lived. All the grace, the beauty, the poetry, had gone out of the majestic river!

MARK TWAIN, *"Old Times on the Mississippi,"* 1875.

"But it is the business of the novel—"

"Ah!" said the other man.

"It is the business of the novel to picture the daily life in the most exact terms possible, with an absolute and clear sense of proportion. As a usual thing, I think, people have absolutely no sense of proportion. Their noses are tight against life, you see. They perceive mountains where there are no mountains, but frequently a great peak appears no larger than a rat trap. An artist sees a dog down the street—well, his eye instantly relates the dog to its surroundings. The dog is proportioned to the buildings and the trees. Whereas, many people can conceive of that dog's tail resting upon a hill top."

"You have often said that the novel is a perspective," observed the other man.

"A perspective, certainly. It is perspective made for the benefit of people who have no true use of their eyes. The novel, in its real meaning, adjusts the proportions. It preserves the balances."

W.D. HOWELLS *as quoted by Stephen Crane, "Fears Realists Must Wait. An Interesting Talk with William Dean Howells." New York Times, October 28, 1894.*

The house of fiction has in short not one window, but a million—a number of possible windows not to be reckoned, rather; every one of which has been pierced, or is still pierceable, in its vast front, by the need of the individual vision and by the pressure of the individual will. These apertures, of dissimilar shape and size, hang so, all together, over the human scene that we might have expected of them a greater sameness of report than we find. They are but windows at the best, mere holes in a dead wall, disconnected, perched aloft; they are not hinged doors opening straight upon life. But they have this mark of their own that at each of them stands a

figure with a pair of eyes, or at least with a field-glass,
which forms, again and again, for observation, a unique
instrument, insuring to the person making use of it an
impression distinct from every other. He and his
neighbors are watching the same show, but one seeing
more where the other sees less, one seeing black where
the other sees white, one seeing big where the other sees
small, one seeing coarse where the other sees fine. And so
on, and so on; there is fortunately no saying on what,
for the particular pair of eyes, the window may not
open; "fortunately" by reason, precisely, of this
incalculability of range. The spreading field, the human
scene, is the "choice of subject"; the pierced aperture,
either broad or balconied or slit-like and low-browed, is
the "literary form"; but they are, singly or together, as
nothing without the posted presence of the watcher—
without, in other words, the consciousness of the artist.
Tell me what the artist is, and I will tell you of what he
has been *conscious.*

HENRY JAMES, *Preface to* The Portrait of a Lady, *1908.*

T HE CONCERN COMMON TO THE FOREGOING STATEMENTS BY
principal American realists is concern for vision.
They point toward a literature which rests upon a particular theory of vision. In a preliminary way, I should define it as: *Realism,* a theory of Common Vision. Though
it would take a very long time to elaborate the helpful
qualifications of that stark phrase, at this point I should
like to emphasize the useful ambiguity of "common." It
may mean "common" as average, ordinary, normal, democratic. It may also mean "common" as shared, general,
normative, perhaps even universal.

The aim here is to make a beginning toward lending

content to "realism" and "realistic." The hope is to enrich the vocabulary of literary discussion by adding precision to key terms. By examining a historical moment of self-proclaimed realism, perhaps we can move from the verifiable ideas and attitudes of "a realism" toward more abstract and generally applicable meanings. The realism I know best is that of American literature of roughly 1860–1910, and I shall therefore take my examples from it.

Historically that realism appears to exhibit six major characteristics. It began as a negative movement with (1) the customary features of a literary revolt and (2) a new notion of reality from which to be critical of its past. It developed (3) a positive method and content, and (4) its own ethical outlook. It (5) involved itself in a major, but losing, battle for American public taste. Finally (6), in its latest stages it turned toward the psychologism which was to succeed it.

We have become accustomed in the past two centuries to the general pattern of a literary revolt. First comes ennui with the worn conventions of overpopular fashions. Yearning for newness leads to youthful cries of back to nature, and Young Turks riot in the pages of little magazines. Something like that happened with the brilliant generation of Americans who became more or less thirty years old in 1870. They were fed up with romanticism. They expended magnificent resources of wit and creative energy to burlesque it out of public countenance. They defined their dearest wishes for expression and artistic success in contradiction to it. They welcomed eagerly a newness which promised to set them free.

To say it briefly, intellectual newness came to this generation in that form of nineteenth-century scientism ordinarily associated with the man Robert Frost once called "John L." Darwin. For this middle generation of American Darwinists, exposed in youth to the old ideal-

6

ism, Thomas Huxley's agnosticism seemed the properest response to the newness. It led them toward a vaguely positivistic factualism. And, insofar as they were writers, it reinforced their ennui to create a burningly reductive antiromanticism. This "negative realism" turned easily to the satiric reduction of romantic, Dionysian egoism and glamor. Henry James may, as he perceived to his chagrin, have "cut the cable" in *The American* and let the balloon of experience float away into the romantic "disconnected and uncontrolled." But in *The Portrait of a Lady* he was soon engaged in the realist's joyous game of shooting down romantic balloons, piercing them through to let the gassy hot air out and drop them back to earth. A like effect was the aim of Mark Twain's unending campaign against "Sir Walter Scottism." Young William Lyon Phelps, interviewing Howells, reported that he never saw a man laugh so consumedly as Howells while numbering the follies of romance. Howells once described the zest of critical warfare as the fun of "banging the Babes of romance about."

The serious side of their antiromantic attitude showed in what became the humanism of these realists. One can distinguish the realist from the romanticist on the one side and the naturalist on the other by precisely this distinction. The romantic, in the long run, is concerned with the ideal, the transcendent, the superhuman. The naturalist is concerned with vast forces, heredity and environment, a world of brute chance, with what we share of animality, with ultimate reduction, the subhuman. As against the romantic, the realist was certainly reductive. There is type significance in the fact that the fathers of Howells and James were Swedenborgians. Both sons had been taught to believe in a double vision according to the doctrine of "correspondence": above every physical existence there hovered spiritual significance, an angel, an essence, an eternal destiny. As agnostics, both in time felt compelled to blot transcendence out from the realm of intellectual fact. Their vision fell from an upward to a level plane where it focused upon man and his life in the world.

Such humanism produced important technical, that is literary, as well as metaphysical and ethical effects. It led realists to deemphasize plot: for them character, the simple, separate person, came to count; not flashing action or terrific fable. By the same token, literary emotional and sentimental heights, what Howells was to call "effectism," were cut down. Obviously it would seem false to make believe that nonsublime people should pretend to superhuman emotions. In realistic hands, the tools of the novelist would be devoted to the main end of bodying forth characters in their habits as they lived. As a corollary there came a shift in their method to what might be called the imploding symbol, to symbols which functioned to intensify inwardly the total effect of a novel, which did not refer outside the novel to general meaning. A second corollary became an emphasis upon contemporaneousness. The historical novel came to be thought a psychological anomaly.

As is already apparent, no serious writer could have rested in mere negations. Burlesquing romance went well in a humor-mad age. But serious literature required a "positive realism," methods developed to express and present the new vision of the common man in his world. The realists' favorite positive technique became what they called the "dramatic method." It demanded the suppression of the "author" from his scene in the novel as the playwright was excluded from all drama except that of "romantic irony" with its deliberately suicidal destruction of illusion. It demanded the creation of "transparent" narrators who seemed never to intrude between

8

the reader and his vision of the characters, who spoke, when "scenes" and "pictures" could not simply be presented, in an unobtrusively "middle" voice. It regarded plot as the account of a breaking in upon and subsequent retreat from an instant of that seamless continuity which is life and so, once more, suppressed plot as much as editors and public would permit.

Devotion to the dramatic method affected symbolism and "effectism," as has been said. But perhaps its most fateful impulse was that toward the development of the theory of the novel. At the beginning of the realists' period, novelistic theory was cruder than neoclassical theory of tragedy. By the period's end, the famous prefaces of Henry James had presented a thoroughly sophisticated theory from which a serious young novelist could derive everything he might need. The heart of that contribution, of course, lay in the development (by, incidentally, a whole generation of major practitioners in a huge, international school) of the techniques and theory of control of fictional narrative through control of "point of view." Novelists so preoccupied with problems of vision were peculiarly prepared to contribute to an understanding of point of view.

With their scorn for the romantically unique, intense, or superhuman, and with their humanistic concern for persons, the American realists sympathized with democracy. Realism as democracy became a significant feature of the literary movement. Increasingly, the writers concentrated on the commonness of the lives of common men. They thought the common significant because it was fresh to literature (that is, never really done before), because it was intrinsically real, and because it was uniquely important from the "universal" side of the implication of "common." They were led in turn to reinterpret the American Dream and use the language of

Emerson and of Whitman without transcendental reference. The realists dreamed not of "the American Adam" but the superiority of the vulgar. When Matthew Arnold foresaw the ultimate damnation of democracy in the absence of distinction from America, Howells rejoiced. If a nation, he remarked, could produce Emerson and Hawthorne, Lincoln, Grant, and Mark Twain and still escape distinction, there was true hope for it. Precisely the same attitudes Twain immortalized in certain adventures of Huck Finn and of Hank Morgan, the Connecticut Yankee. And, after his fashion, Henry James expressed cognate perceptions in portraits of that most contemptible of men, the Europeanized American.

The evolution of the travel book and of the perceptions of cultural relativity which the practice of travel writing engendered in the writers helped give rise to realism, and thereafter a natural concern of the realist was the international theme. Henry James on the Europeanized American, Howells's exploration of the "conventional-unconventional" conflict, and Twain's transmutation of the frontier humorist's war against the Eastern snob all came to the same point. Of necessity, the realist fought snobbery and factitious aristocracy. In doing so he rang every imaginable change upon the theme of the Innocent Abroad. We are far from having exhausted the meaning inherent in the famous opposed curves of the attitudes of James and Twain toward American values, early Twain against early James and late against late. And Howells, sharing with and often anticipating both, arrived at his visions of Tolstoi and Altruria in a fascinating kind of mediation between them.

A fourth characteristic of this American realism was its moral vision. As one may see in the familiar writings of Howells and James—*The Rise of Silas Lapham,* "The

Beast in the Jungle"—essential to their moral vision was an active disbelief in the health or safety of romantic individualism, of Dionysian self-assertion. The same sense gives resonance to Huck Finn's famous decision to go to hell for Nigger Jim. Conformity to the code of Tom Sawyer's misshapen "civilization" would have brought Huck the sensations of "salvation" for his "ornery" soul and the comfort of self-respect for his "low-down" and outcast character. He had almost chosen respectable self-identity and the sanction to stand upright in an individualistic culture. Instead, he chose damnation: that is, solidarity (as Edward Bellamy would call his religion beyond egotism) or "complicity," as Howells repeatedly termed it, with Jim—in hell, if necessary. A like self-sacrifice accords Jim his climactic meed of heroism when he steps out of hiding, presumably into bondage again if not death by torture, when the frantic doctor calls for aid to wounded Tom Sawyer.

These were the attitudes, consciously antiromantic, which led Stephen Crane to conclude that, "The final wall of the wise man's thought . . . is Human Kindness of course." Their reduction (at least in nasal altitude) of morality from sublimity to solidarity made the common vision appear essential to a right grasp of life. Therefore Howells announced that a bad novel was a school of crime. And Hjalmar Hjorth Boyesen, with Scandinavian solemnity, backed him up by arguing that "romance" deprives its devotees of "sound standards of judgement," whereas realism reveals "the significance of common facts and events . . . the forces that govern the world . . . and the logic of life."

Their moral vision reinforced the realists' affinities for democracy and contemporaneousness and brought them toward effective insights into the human problems of the historically unique industrial culture forming around them. Those insights stimulated their alliances with the growing sentiment of reform. The preservation and extension of democracy, Populism, Progressivism, Nationalism (Bellamy's, that is), unions and the labor movement, socialism, anti-imperialism, and, perhaps most permanently, a long-continuing critical examination of the American Business Mind, occupied in various ways much of the thought and creative inquiry of the American realists as their movement matured. Even Henry James, most obviously with *The Princess Casamassima* and "The Jolly Corner," took his part.

Of the long and little-understood international critical fight of the era, the Realism War in its American aspect, it is probably not necessary to say a great deal. The realists fought to capture American taste from romanticism, lost, and left romanticism established, dominant as it has been since the foundation of the Republic and, in spite of all resistance, in what appears to be our native mold. The gains of their warfare were a considerable contribution to the theory of the novel and a legacy of models and of challenge which would substantially affect novelists to come.

Finally, since some sort of change seems to be historically inevitable, it was proper that American realism should develop in such a way as to prepare for its own succession. The writers moved toward an increasingly psychological realism, propelled by two major forces. One of these was the displacement of positivism from its dominance of late nineteenth-century thought. A decade like the nineties, which began with William James's *Psychology* and ended with the unleashing of those electronic factors in physical thought which produced Henry Adams's image of "himself lying in the Gallery of Machines at the Great Exposition of 1900, his historical neck broken by the sudden irruption of forces totally new,"

12

was bound to loosen the grip of positivism on the imagination. A second force, however, arose from the practices of realistic fiction itself. The more one confronted the mystery of persons living out their fates and struggling toward death, the more his scrutiny turned from the outward sign to the inward process. Howells noticed in 1903, when he was writing a novel Freudian in everything but specifically Viennese terminology, that all the realists had been turning to psychology. Indeed, many had been flirting with psychic phenomena as far-flung as the claims of spiritualism. What he did not seem to notice was that he himself had been working in psychological realism since he began *The Shadow of a Dream* in 1889.

Obviously, however, the methods and angles of vision of realism could not be finally satisfactory for the exploration of psychology. The more one moved from the seen toward the unseeable, from the common toward the private vision, the more other methods appealed. The movement toward symbolism of the late James was as natural as the movement into stream of consciousness for Joyce. Thus realism prepared the way for its succession.

One must, it goes without saying, be aware that the Americans did not work in isolation. They participated in a huge, though ill-defined, international realistic school. To the best of my knowledge, no one has yet essayed to study the figure of late nineteenth-century international realism, though obviously such names as those of Flaubert, Zola, and Daudet in France; Turgenev, Tolstoi, Dostoevski, Gogol in Russia; Galdós, Palacio Valdés, and Pardo-Bazan in Spain; Björnson, Ibsen, and Brandes in Scandinavia; Hauptmann in Germany, Verga in Italy, Hardy and then Bennett and Galsworthy in England, stand out. I could not pretend to discuss the grand pattern. But perhaps I can propose certain general considerations, more or less abstracted from the American experience, for clarifying the terms "realism" and "realistic."

As a beginning, I wish to propose two distinctions which I should like to make precise. The first is to distinguish between "realism" as a literary mode and "reality" in every extraliterary sense. The second is to distinguish the literary situation in which apparently realistic means have been employed to secure final, total effects which are not realistic from the work which does finally, in totality, achieve realism. Ultimately, I shall propose a general definition of realism which might survive these distinctions.

Most ordinary, dictionary definitions of realism are circular. Realism, they say, deals with what is real (if not merely with what is unpleasant). The OED is a notorious offender in this respect, and the Webster International says: "In art and literature, fidelity to nature or to real life." Apart from bald circularity, there are several objections to such definitions. They provide no means of distinguishing realistic from other literature. We do not have, and are not likely soon to achieve, general agreement about the nature of reality—the qualities of "nature" and "real life." Furthermore, such questions are metaphysical and philosophical, and we are after a literary definition. We need to discard the notion that realism must rest upon a discarded nineteenth-century and vaguely positivistic factualism—or, indeed, rest upon any philosophical realism—and look further.

Questions of definition in literary studies are customarily (and I think rightly) referred to the effects of literature upon the reader. Consideration of such an essentially psychological question sometimes leads to a definition in which literature is called "realistic" because it is so vivid, powerful, profound, or exact in its effect upon the receiving imagination that it "seems real." But this definition, I think, confuses "realism" with literary success. The essence of literary art is to "seem real" in the sense of captivating the reader's imagination, no matter what the qualities of the experience to which imagination is led in the chains of art. That way, all true literature becomes "realistic." But whatever means everything means nothing. "Realism" as a term is destroyed. If it is to have any viable critical use, the term must distinguish some kind of true, of successful, literature from other kinds. The same dead end is reached by the argument that "realism" should be taken to mean "faithful to the writer's unique and personal sense of reality." Every sound expressive success, regardless of variances among authors' faiths and visions, would become "realistic." We must return to the problem of psychological effect, but for the present let us affirm that literary realism has nothing special to do with "reality" as such.

In the present posture of general knowledge, including that of some fundamental sciences, formidable intellectual difficulties stand in the way of proposing to "imitate nature" or "transcribe reality." As Werner Heisenberg concluded, at the epistemological foundations of modern physics Platonism seems to have reclaimed its power. In the end phenomena elude our grasp. We can know not themselves but only ideas of them, and the very injection of an idea into a natural process for purposes of investigation appears so to alter the process as to make it impossible to be sure what the realities unobserved might be.

To say "process" introduces still more unsettling questions about imitating nature: which nature? In social and psychological as well as physical realms we now see no solid, autonomous "fact." Instead there appear complex, if not, for practical purposes, endlessly receding grades of flowing abstraction. Ancient rational categories melt to flux. The further one follows, the more remote from common human, or even uncommon personal, experience grow the unimaginably complicated processes. And they are always emergent, always "becoming." They "arrive" only wherever we call a halt by arbitrary intellectual fiat. Still worse, when, for purposes of art or knowledge, we call the halt, that arrest is made, that stop occurs, not infrequently past any point at which things remain available to the ways we have of imagining experience. No telling how much "reality" altogether outruns us. The problem of what then to make of what we have imagined, or of what to do with ourselves in relation to it, becomes acute.

It is probably not profitable to spin out illustrations of such problems. They inhere in any consideration of the peeling layers of the means one possesses for understanding the chair he sits in. The work of understanding the chair rises in one direction at last into the mysteries of the psychological origins of form; or in another direction at last to the baffling physical concept of matter as a swirl of energy when energy is not quite definable; or in yet another direction at last toward the uncontrollable question of why, culturally, there should be chairs when nothing biological demands them. One loses, ultimately, all sense of direct connection to experience.

Clearly we are now in the way of developing art which runs likewise "free" of experience. It is not our purpose here to explore such art, however. We are to look toward those kinds of thought and art, together with the problems of understanding which lie behind them, which may help us toward a definition of realism. Realism is obviously a kind of art which does deal with experience, even common and shared, not highly personal or esoteric experience. The question is, how?

16

Let us turn on to a perhaps useful distinction between "realism" and "verisimilitude." It is my impression that much confusion in the discussion of realism has been caused by failure to attend to the difference between the effect of one part of a work of literature and the effect of the whole. Because, for instance, there are moments of strategic attention to homely detail in *The Faerie Queene* and in *Henry IV,* Part I, it is sometimes said that they are realistic. They are in total effect heroic, chivalric, exotic, rather romantic, and, in the case of *The Faerie Queene,* allegorical-fantastic: great works, but not realism.

The same point might be made by examining such very different pieces as the opening pages of *Gulliver's Travels* and Poe's famous tale "The Descent into the Maelstrom." In Swift's opening there is a wonderfully "voiced" and detailed account of the ordinary career of a wilful lad who became a commonplace ship's surgeon. We are led comfortably into an apparently normal memoir of travel and adventure by sea, suspicion at rest, disbelief suspended. And all at once we find ourselves in Lilliput. The tactic is obvious. In Poe's tale we are drawn with the narrator into a scene of horror, hanging with his ship on the wall of a mammoth whirlpool down the sides of which we may slip inexorably to destruction as gravity slowly overcomes centrifugal force. Both the unity and Gothic effect of the tale demand, however, that the narrator shall escape while we, at least through the duration of the tale, shall believe in his escape. How to do this? Poe resorts to a brilliantly precise description of just how it was that objects whirled and swam, sank or stayed up in the maelstrom. We see with the narrator that he *must* lash himself to a barrel and leap into the torrential wall of water, abandoning his fear-paralyzed brother to destruction with the heavy ship. The total effect is one of fantastic horror and release, Gothicism at its best.

If one were to take the moments of what might look like realism in all four works to authorize calling the works realistic, he would have lost, at least to that extent, the grounds for differentiating among them. Yet it is clearly important critically to avoid confounding *The Faerie Queene, Henry IV,* Part I, *Gulliver's Travels,* and "The Descent into the Maelstrom." To call them all realistic would be to obscure the essential literary qualities of each; for each has as the essential qualities of its greatness, qualities not realistic. Hence the usefulness of distinguishing local, partial, even fragmentary uses of realistic effects to contribute to what will in the long run and total effect be nonrealistic, from what achieves realism in final effect. The partial or local effects I would call "verisimilitude," reserving the word "realism" for the other.

What, then, to come finally to the point, should be called "realism"? If this were easy to answer, there would have been no excuse for all the prologue. It is certainly not, and especially across patterns of culture or down historical perspectives, easy. By way of attempting an answer, I wish to recur to the earliest pages of this discussion and suggest that literary realism be seen as dependent upon a theory of common vision. That theory rests upon the combination of a theory of literary art with an amateur theory of perception.

First, the theory of common vision assumes that art-technical (the words of the text on the page in their patterns) arouses in the reader art as experience by impelling his imagination to create that experience subjectively. It observes that there is some, presently obscure, relationship between the experience a reader gets (or can make) from "non-art," what we call "life," and the experience he derives from art. It sees that there are many varieties of both orders of experience and that in some meaningful sense art-experiences and non-art experiences can be paired as with A to A-1, B to B-1, etc. The difference between A and A-1 arises from the great difference in what occasions each; their likeness arises from their relating to the same category of subjective effect. For instance, one sees a view, sees a painting, reads a poetic description: and "feels" landscape. One "sees" a ghost, he sees *Hamlet,* he reads *Hamlet.* One eats at a cafeteria, he reads of so eating. It is not to be doubted that art as technique will strategically have shaped art-experience. We can apparently not quite know how that non-art experience occurs which may range from foggy undifferentiatedness to something explosive or fateful. The point to be clung to is that there persistently are varietal likenesses between instances of the two orders of experience. That is why one should be loath to deny relationship between literature and "reality" even while observing all the caveats noted earlier.

It might therefore be possible to propose a positive and general definition of realism as representing the art-variety of a "real" order of non-art experience—an order, that is, which even those who held to deeply opposed temperamental and metaphysical notions of ultimate reality might agree to accept as "real" in some useful and common, even though minimal, sense. That variety I should propose to be the socially agreed upon "common vision" which permits ordinary processes of law and social control to succeed, creates the possibility of games, makes most technical, economic, and even educational enterprises possible. That world of the common vision is, indeed, what is ordinarily referred to as "reality." But, of course, it has not been reality for many people of the past as it is not for many—and especially for many artists—

today. It could not finally serve, that is, for any true Idealist, or Humean sceptic, or Existentialist, or mystic, Zen, or hippie thinker.

The world of common vision does certainly not in itself encompass all the varieties of "reality" available to art experience. But it certainly is, on the other hand, in fact one sort of reality common to almost everybody. It provides the ground for one kind, a dominant variety, of non-art experience. There must surely be a variety of art-experience cognate to the world of common vision. Regardless, then, of whether it is absolutely so or not, what usually appears to be "reality" is experience which it appears that we share with other people. We check the content and qualities of our experience with the experience of others to see whether ours is "real" or not. With some orders of experience we check so automatically that it never occurs to us to ask whether we ought to, whether it is valid to check with others. When doubt strikes us with regard to the commonness of most experience, we fear we may be retreating from reality into fantasy.

And of course it is in the areas of experience which are most socially verifiable that we feel ourselves most shared and sharing. In a game the ball is either caught or not caught—and the resultant exultation or dejection depends altogether on group-related gambling emotions. The like holds true for the law or politics; they also entirely depend on community of experience, on the experience of reality as common vision.

So it is just upon this question of the possibility of experience socially based upon common vision that the possibility of literary realism hangs. If the novelist can through the illusions of his art induce imaginative experience within his reader consonant with the reader's ordinary communal experience, then intriguing possibilities appear. There can be a literature peculiarly potent in its appeal to some of the sanest and most useful processes of the human mind. From certain practical and moral points of view, that should be a literature uniquely valuable—for, if it were successful as art, done with esthetic force, conceived by the eye of a necessarily supersensitive observer, the illusion of experience, the "sense of life" conveyed could not fail to be deeply instructive. The power of art to create experience more intense, more sharply defined and vivid, more satisfactorily shaped than the experience people can normally create for themselves would be lent to the deepening and enhancement of the common vision. Such literature would make us better citizens, more loyal in our loves, more perceptive in critique, more faithful to perspectives clearly seen.

Such a literature would be time and culture bound of course. Especially concerned with persons in their relations with other persons, it would tend to be democratic. In order to preserve its integrity as art rather than essay or sermon, it would have to forswear the vatic anarchies of "organicism" and concentrate hard on problems of form. It would learn to master the arts of creating illusions of objectivity and impartiality, abjuring the cult of artistic personality and the temptation to romantic irony.

All these, and perhaps other, features would go to make a particular kind of literary method and effect. The importance of the kind would, as with all kinds, depend largely on the power of its practitioner to achieve artistic success—the strong command of the reader's imagination—by its method. In this respect the kind would be no different from any other. The whole argument here is to show that the literary art of the common vision deserves recognition as a kind and is, theoretically as well as historically, entitled to the name of realism.

21

Finally, I should like to suggest that if we meant the foregoing things by "realism" and "reality" we could justify the nineteenth-century realists outside and beyond the conventions of their time and thought—forward into the present and backward as far as we know art. So doing, we could still grasp the relevant patterns and call what seems to conform to these patterns "realism." Admittedly, cross-cultural problems might become very difficult. For us the difficulties of imagining our way into the realisms of cultures which take magic, witchcraft, or mythology as ordinarily operative can be great. So too our difficulties with bygone science and scientism. For instance, astrology, the psychology of humours, phrenology, or even Zolaistic naturalism are hard for us to take as matters of the common vision. They must be defined socially in their proper contexts by mighty efforts of the historical or the cross-cultural imagination.

But there may be valuable rewards for such efforts. The thrill of insight and the power of command through a knowledgeable sympathy with men of other times, other places, may accompany, through the ambiguity of "common" as universal, a new grasp of those human universals which we are told some cultural anthropologists are beginning to find in human nature. Thus we might recover one of the traditional glories of the study of literature.

2 / Three Sensibilities:

Romancer, Realist,

Naturalist

AT THE GAME OF CULTURAL DEFINITIONS, THE PLURALIST almost always wins. Time with its deaths and innovations plays on his side. The burdens of proof fall heavily on the shoulders of his antagonist. The pluralist always has the advantage of the terrible difficulty, perhaps at last the impossibility, encountered by the unitary definer in bridging the incongruities which gape between intellectual generalization and the uniqueness of actual events in culture—like a work of fiction, for instance. Perhaps it makes another and easier sense, certainly it comes closer to the actual cultural phenomena of the author, the book, and the reader, to consider modes of sensibility. Romancer, realist, and naturalist are easier to understand as persons, experiencing and expressing different sensibilities, than as lay figures standing for "isms."

I

IN PHRASES JUSTLY FAMOUS, NATHANIEL HAWthorne apologized for his work by explaining himself as a Romancer. Such a man's work, he said, might "claim a certain latitude, both as to its fashion and material." If he wishes, "he may so manage his atmospherical medium as to bring out or mellow the lights and deepen and enrich the shadows of the picture." At his peril and discretion, he may deal in "the Marvellous." Above all, Hawthorne pleaded, "atmosphere is what the American romancer needs." The "common-place prosperity in broad and simple daylight" which he thought "happily" the American condition, might long constrict the imagination of the artist: "Romance and poetry, ivy, lichens, and wall-flowers need ruin to make them grow."

It was therefore elevation, mystery, terror, ideality, sublimity, and the weird which New England lacked: some sense of a "Faery Land, so like the real world, that in a suitable remoteness, one cannot well tell the difference, but with an atmosphere of strange enchantment, beheld through which the inhabitants have a propriety of their own." For Hawthorne, of course, the romancer's wild, strange world was subject to laws, but only two. The romance "as a work of art" must "rigidly subject itself to laws" esthetic; and "it sins unpardonably so far as it may swerve aside from the truth of the human heart"—laws of sentiment, taste and choice: ultimately moral laws; but proximately modes of sensibility.

Deeper in the psyche than ideas, perhaps a source for them, certainly a major determinant of our choice of one possible idea in favor of another, sensibility is more than "feelings," emotion. It connotes tact, a feeling for life, a way of taking events and making experience, a ground for life-style and at last for morality.

Among American romancers Hawthorne was not only the mage, the Essex wizard, the best of artists. He was also most typical because most balanced and inclusive. He held in a fine, mysterious equilibrium the two central urges of sensibility which raged to tear the

American romancer apart. Both Dionysian, both compel-
ling the sensibility toward superhuman vision, faith, and
emotion, they pulled against each other like wild horses:
Autonomy against Ideality.

Poe's was superbly the autonomous sensibility
among American romancers:

> Our flowers are merely—flowers,
> And the shadow of thy perfect bliss
> Is the sunshine of ours.

> If I could dwell
> Where Israfel
> Hath dwelt, and he where I,
> He might not sing so wildly well
> A mortal melody,
> While a bolder note than this might swell
> From my lyre within the sky.

Anything less, the mere knowledge of mortal contin-
gency, brought on that vision of evil, thundering "eternal
Condor years" of anguish, against which the artist had
only his defiant fist to raise above his stricken brow and
his fleeting moment of peace and creative power to prove
once more his angelic identity and exile from heaven.

Emerson and Thoreau, on the opposite shore,
scorned an autonomy which could not transcend anguish
and lose itself in the One."Give all to love;/ Obey thy
heart;/ . . . Leave all for love;" said Emerson, sad in the
sceptic's knowledge that in this world of sweets and sours
no sacrifice so utter, no act so Dionysian but limit, time,
and blight would transform it. Yet, welcome the change,
cried mystic Waldo; it may open the watergates and let
the Oversoul flow in:

> Though thou loved her as thyself,
> As a self of purer clay,
> Though her parting dims the day,
> Stealing grace from all alive;

> Heartily know,
> When half-gods go,
> The gods arrive.

And thus when the ecstasy of "Spring" comes to *Walden* we are treated to Mr. Thoreau's sermon on Easter:

> In a pleasant spring morning all men's sins are forgiven. . . . Through our own recovered innocence we discern the innocence of our neighbors. . . . Ah! I have penetrated to those meadows on the morning of many a first spring day . . . when the wild river valley and the woods were bathed in so pure and bright a light as would have waked the dead, if they had been slumbering in their graves, as some suppose. There needs no stronger proof of immortality. All things must live in such a light. O Death, where was thy sting? O Grave, where was thy victory, then?

All things considered, "The impression made on a wise man is that of universal innocence. Poison is not poisonous after all, nor are any wounds fatal. Compassion is a very untenable ground."

Ishmael's recollections of the war between Autonomy and Ideality aboard and alongside the *Pequod* made for great romance. So did the account of that same war within the hearts of a minister, a physician, and a woman of Old Salem. But of course there were a great many considerations more than two for the American romancer, and his imagination played endlessly Protean, shape-shifting dramas with them all. To begin to name and grade considerations or list the *dramatis personae* is to lift them up toward the thin atmosphere of the "isms," however, and we are out for sensibility. Is there a work short enough to consider which offers a blend and balance of the varieties of romantic sensibility in American fiction? I think there is: in one of the best yet rather seldom studied of the short stories of Hawthorne, "The Artist of the Beautiful."

This extraordinary tale looks forward to Clemens and Howells and then to Willa Cather and Sherwood Anderson in its treatment of the small town and the anguish of a sensitive, creative soul in conflict with petty, indurated "practicality." Owen Warland, an artisan faithful to "the grand object of a watchmaker's business . . . the measurement of time" with its attendant mysteries, finds himself called to "a new development of the love of the beautiful, such as might have made him a poet, a painter, or a sculptor, and which was as completely refined from all utilitarian coarseness as it could have been in either of the fine arts." Warland's work "seemed to aim at the hidden mysteries of mechanism. But it was always for purposes of grace, and never with any mockery of the useful." Steam engines made him sick. He discovered, at length, that the calling of his heart and mind was to accomplish what Nature had neglected, to spiritualize machinery.

The theme of a transcendent watchmaker answered of course to established American impulses in romantic sensibility. Emerson had waxed oratorical in the peroration to "The American Scholar":

> . . . I embrace the common, I explore and sit at the feet of the familiar, the low. . . . What would we really know the meaning of ? The meal in the firkin; the milk in the pan; the ballad in the street; the news of the boat; the glance of the eye; the form and gait of the body;—show me the ultimate reason of these matters; show me the sublime presence of the highest spiritual cause lurking, as always it does lurk, in these suburbs and extremities of nature; let me see every trifle bursting with the polarity that ranges it instantly on an eternal law.

One might easily line out the rhetorical units and smuggle them into *Leaves of Grass*. At least partly in answer to the same impulse Melville undertook to mythologize a whale ship's captain and crew.

Hawthorne wrote his story in three basic movements capped by a fine climactic scene. The first movement sets the contrasts and conflicts between the artist of the beautiful and the world. Owen is in love with Annie, daughter of his retired master, Peter Hovenden; and old Peter incarnates the Coleridgean "understanding," the cold, practical, sceptical shrewdness which thrives in this present physical world because it can see no further. Peter scorns Owen and supports his rival for Annie's hand, mighty Robert Danforth, the blacksmith: "it is a good and wholesome thing to depend upon main strength and reality, and to earn one's bread with the bare and brawny arm of a blacksmith," cries Peter.

But the very atmosphere of the smith bewilders and enfeebles slender, sensitive Warland. "His hard, brute force darkens and confuses the spiritual element within me," says the artist, and with a slip of the finger-tips he ruins the work of months. "Thus it is," comments the narrator in summing up the first movement of the tale,

> that ideas, which grow up within the imagination and appear so lovely to it and of a value beyond whatever men call valuable, are exposed to be shattered and annihilated by contact with the practical. It is requisite for the ideal artist to possess a force of character that seems hardly compatible with its delicacy; he must keep faith in himself while the incredulous world assails him in utter disbelief; he must stand up against mankind and be his own sole disciple, both as respects his genius and the objects to which it is directed.

The second and third movements of "The Artist of the Beautiful" trace Warland's repeated rises to inspiration and falls to failure, alienation, and despair. Annie Hovenden, half understanding, provides him with a phrase for his quest, "the notion of putting spirit into machinery." For a moment he thinks he has found "the sympathy" which might deliver him from the agony of the "sensation of moral cold" in the world which tortures every prophetic or creative soul. But in the same breath Annie carelessly, playfully destroys with the touch of her needle-point his latest experiment. Crushed together with his creation, Warland takes to drink until rescued by Nature. A "splendid butterfly" enters the tavern and Owen rises, to drink no more. " 'Ah,' " he exclaims, 'are you alive again, child of the sun . . . ?' It might be fancied that the bright butterfly, which had come so spirit-like into the window as Owen sat with the rude revellers, was indeed a spirit commissioned to recall him to the pure, ideal life that had so etherealized him among men."

Crushed a third time by Annie's marriage to the smith, Warland comes to prefigure the character who would haunt the imaginations of midwestern writers like Howells, Twain, and Willa Cather and whom Sherwood Anderson would call "grotesques." But he recovers. Hawthorne does not presume to tell us how Warland broke through to his "instant of solitary triumph." He foreshortens that mystery to deliver us upon the scene at Robert Danforth's home, where the artist of the beautiful comes to deliver his present to the pair so long wedded they have a crawling baby who is the spiritual spit and image of Peter Hovenden.

The irony with which the tale treats the domestic scene inverts the usual response of a romancer's sensibility to themes of hearth and home; in this story, however, irony is not only appropriate but necessary to the theme. To Annie the artist presents for a "bridal gift" his creation: "this spiritualized mechanism, this harmony of motion, this mystery of beauty." When Annie opens its box there flies out "Nature's ideal butterfly . . . realized in all its perfection, in perfect beauty." Alive, it glows with spiritual light and flies, yet Owen made it. He does not tell the family that he has given Annie "a gem of art that a monarch would have purchased with honors and abundant wealth, and have treasured it among the jewels of his kingdom as the most unique and wondrous of them all. . . . the artist smiled and kept the secret to himself."

And he watches in fascination. Alive with the essence of Owen's intellect, imagination, sensibility, and soul, the butterfly is sensitive to spiritual vibrations. Contact with Peter Hovenden almost kills it. Contact with the baby makes it sparkle and grow dim alternately. When it tries to return to the artist, he declines: it has gone forth from his heart and may not return. Confused, the butterfly hovers near Peter Hovenden's grandson and is snatched to destruction. Annie screams. Old Peter laughs in scorn. In the baby's palm the blacksmith finds "a small heap of glittering fragments, whence the mystery of beauty had fled forever."

But Owen Warland? Was the artist of the beautiful crushed again? Did he despair? Not at all:

> . . . he looked placidly at what seemed the ruin of his life's labor, and which was yet no ruin. He had caught a far other butterfly than this. When the artist rose high enough to achieve the beautiful, the symbol by which he made it perceptible to mortal senses became of little value in his eyes while his spirit possessed itself in the enjoyment of the reality.

The connections of "The Artist of the Beautiful" to many varieties of the romantic sensibility are numerous, sometimes startling. If the sentiment of hearth and home is inverted and missing are the delights of the exotic, the sublime and terrible, the wild, and the simple, and most of romantic politics, everything else is there. The story rather astonishingly connects Poe to Thoreau. An estranged, betrayed, dejected Autonom, a Byronic loser, the artist of the beautiful brings in his life as a tribute "For Annie." But the story rebukes self-pity. Warland can conclude with Thoreau that compassion is a doctrine suspect if even tenable in a world which may be transcended to spiritual triumph. Like Thoreau's "artist in the city of Kouroo," Warland found that though life might pass him by, penetration to the ideal liberated him from the ego and its penalties. "The Artist of the Beautiful" seems to ignore the ordinary Hawthornian ethics of compassion and sympathy in its concentration on an Emersonian act of transcendence through art. But Hawthorne had found the cord of esthetic insight which bound Emerson to Melville. He had also expressed precisely that ideal of esthetic sensibility in romance against which the sensibility of a realist would find it essential to revolt.

I I

ESPECIALLY AS REGARDS HAWTHORNE, THE REALISTS would obviously have preferred to have it some other way; but they had to begin to define themselves in revolution and attack. It is perhaps easiest to get at a result which was a good deal more than metaphysical by recalling one of that rebellion's religious aspects. One can even start from that somehow improbable fact that the fathers of Howells and the Jameses were both Swedenborgians— adherents of a religion devoted to the doctrine of correspondence. "Correspondence" is the idea that reality is double, or, as Emerson said in his famous proposals concerning "Words" in *Nature,* natural facts are symbols of spiritual facts. Where the fathers were dualists, the sons became agnostics. And from agnostic vision the old world of spirit simply disappeared. Agnostics did not deny the possibility of spiritual reality; indeed, they could be observed continually pressing to find whether it might somehow be restored. But the spiritual was not to be seen. Their faith was reduced. The difference between Hawthorne's butterfly and Howells's "ideal grasshopper" was that between vital ideality and dead convention.

Of course, some process of reduction became virtually the history of the modernizing mind—reduction, reduction: down and down the ladder. As Robert Frost recalled in "The White-Tailed Hornet," the history of modern thought is like the old Russian legend about people in a sledge pursued by wolves. We have thrown one faith after another to the wolves until at last, as Frost said, "Nothing but fallibility was left us." Reduction in possibility of belief and possibility of vision from the spiritual to the human was the agnostic's fate. It was also the realist's fate. Where the old deist-democrat had asserted the central importance of man's sufficient reason, and where the romantic democrat had asserted the sacredness of man's intuitive access to truth, beauty, and goodness, the realist was forced to doubt the sufficiency of reason and the existence both of noumena and of any human capacity to apprehend them should they exist. When Hawthorne looked at character, he saw symbolic value; and symbolic value was spiritual. To the vision of Howells or Crane, characters are valuable as persons, for their irreducible humanity. A failed spiritualist, yet no monist, the realist become humane.

And for the realist as for all artists, sensibility outranked mere ideas. The common itself and the value of the common began to fascinate. It is too much overlooked in *Adventures of Huckleberry Finn* that there morality depends upon the value of the common, the simple, separate person. In contradistinction from Whitman, for

Twain, as for realists generally, the simple separate person had become now no more than common and personal. He was a *simple, separate, person* ultimately valuable for personhood alone. Nothing further existed to the eye and touch of a realist. Therefore, one major realistic tendency was to cut down superexperience by critical irony, to undercut the romancer's yen to elevate and inflate experience—to bring it down to the plane of common humanity. Perhaps it was even in part the pain of nostalgia for vanished faith that urged the sensibility of the realist to hostility against the romancer's afflatus. And perhaps a compensating affection for the common, unadorned and immitigable, helped urge the realist to fictional representation of the new world his disillusioned heart had come to love.

If the realist in practice often defined his vision by the malice with which he exposed to satiric or ironic destruction the expectations of readers trained to romantic sensibility, he murdered for love. After Darwin, what forgiveness? Down the neoromantic road pioneered the pimping footprints of Bret Harte. There were left to the realist the chances for honesty: for integrity in vision, integrity in form and effect, and the chance to love the one surely visible reality, common humanity. The point of the realist's affection has diminished in neither force nor importance during a century past. C. P. Snow put it plainly to the University of Michigan class of 1963:

> We have got to fall back with great simplicity on the fact that the essence of each human person is equivalent to the essence of each other human person. Some of us can do tricks which others can't. Most people have their excellences. But none of that matters besides the fact that each of us is human. Unless we hold to that, hold to it patiently, hold that the essence of human beings is more important than their politics, their color, their race, hold that the

resemblances between each of us are incomparably more important than the differences, then there is no hope for us.

Out of the realist's sensibility, then, his art arose as a matter first of taste and then of esthetics and morality. His esthetic contained, as its practitioners revealed, a double potential. On the one side arose the democrats, fusing the esthetic of the "common vision" with agnostic individualism to reinterpret the Jeffersonian tradition. They became unsparing enemies of whatever threatened the democratic person and so, by fairly obvious steps, militant protesters against the threats of industrialization, urbanization, and the cultural dislocations of their age, which we inherit. Despite his politics, the greatest of democrats was Mark Twain, though the local color realists and after them the "Chicago School" constituted a kind of submovement. The social reformers constituted another.

On the other hand there stood Henry James, with an esthetic which also easily became a morality. It was equally realistic, equally concerned for persons and their integrity, but politically irrelevant. For James realism was essentially an artistic means for presenting valid impressions of life to his reader. For him realism readily became method, as in that famous remark of Picasso, "We all know that art is not truth. Art is a lie that makes us realize truth—at least the truth that is given to us to understand. . . ." James was at one with the democrats in insisting on the importance of a human, personal outlook from one's particular window pierced through the walls of the house of fiction and giving upon an outwardly factual life. That life the realist felt to be commonly available in its intrinsic reality of existence to everyone, limited only by the boundaries of perspective afforded by his special niche.

But James the artist knew that a writer could not place life, or his vision of it, directly upon a page. As realist, the writer had neither more nor less resource than other artists. Like every artist he was dependent upon the techniques of art to move the imagination of his reader. And his techniques were as illusionary as those of the wildest purveyor of sheer fantasy. The problem, then, was to find methods of so controlling the necessary illusion as to give the reader the right impression of life. Obviously the vision must be translated into illusions and the illusions must convey the impression to the reader before there could be realistic art. The great question was how to arrive at the right illusions and how to preserve the integrity of the total illusion which constituted the novel itself so as to achieve the central effect. With all his genius, James worked from the inspiration of Turgenev and his "dramatic method" until he created that precision in the theory and variable practice of controlling fictional point of view which constitutes his unparalleled contribution to the art of the novel. In criticism as well as practice he developed the ideal of responsibility to the novel as a form of art which brought serious fiction to its first entire fruition.

But the substance, the thing sensed in common humanity by the nerves of the realist, was in the end always something moral. As the object was human the issue was moral. Issues of value, what to do, how to do it, and the reasons why, the realist felt central to every concern affecting common, observable, experientially knowable and communicable humanity. Humanism demanded moral vision, moral seriousness.

Morality, however, to the realist's sense must never be moralized, never be interpreted abstractly. It had to be observed on the wing, in the fleeting circumstances of personal life expressed in the particular case of a charac-

35

ter responsibly portrayed, understood, responded to. It could be moralized only as the imagination of a reader grasped the issue and saw how, perhaps, it might illuminate his personal experience. The literature of realism became, therefore, a literature of moral illumination, a literature of revelation. The sensibility of the realist prized insight most. The grasp of character and its moral significance became his mode of the imagination. And his art, his craft, prized above all else expertise in revelation.

Two otherwise vastly different examples demonstrate the foregoing generalization by their focus upon revelation: Mark Twain's first achievement in literature, "A True Story"; Henry James's almost too carelessly mature masterwork, "The Beast in the Jungle." Twain's piece, "A True Story Repeated Word for Word as I Heard It," became a turning point in his career. And, if there were no other, Twain's story could be used as the classic example of positive achievement in a new mode of American fiction. Howells, who had accepted "A True Story" for the *Atlantic,* jumped at the chance to explain its significance when *Sketches Old and New* appeared in 1875. "A True Story" Howells called "the most perfect piece of work in the book." He mocked the "shyness of an enlightened and independent press" for muffing its point in reviewing the November 1874 *Atlantic:*

> Not above two or three notices out of hundreds recognized "A True Story" for what it was—namely, a study of character as true as life itself, strong, tender, and most movingly pathetic in its perfect fidelity to the tragic fact.... The rugged truth of the sketch leaves all other stories of slave life infinitely far behind, and reveals a gift in the author for the simple, dramatic report of reality which we have seen equalled in no other American writer.

Without possibly being aware of the fact, Howells had fired an opening skirmisher's shot in what within a dozen years or so would be the full-scale Realism War.

The differences between "The Artist of the Beautiful" and "A True Story" could hardly be more radical. Hawthorne's climactic scene is almost twice as long as Twain's whole piece. Hawthorne centers upon the triumph fantasy of a thwarted artist and redeems it by a symbolic transformation pointing to supernal value, a transformation he can achieve only through editorial intervention. "A True Story" is in the last degree dramatic. The narrator, "Mr. C_____," is set up as a stooge or straight man, the idiot at large, so "Aunt Rachel," a magnificent black woman, can tell her story. Once she begins —"Has I had any trouble? Mister C___, I's gwyne to tell you, den I leave it to you"—all the words are hers; and she has established the dramatic point: interpretation will be left to us.

Aunt Rachel's story is simple, and she tells it with swift pace. Born a slave, she had a husband and seven children in Virginia. But when "ole mistis" went broke, the slaves were sold at auction, the family dispersed. Though Rachel had set her heart on recovering at least Henry, her youngest, she had no success until he appeared, during the War, as a black soldier attached to the Union headquarters where Rachel worked as a cook. The moving episode, ancient as folktale, presents the recognition motifs by which the long-separated mother and son discover each other. The key is a ranting, angry formula which Rachel had inherited from her mother: "Look-a-heah! I want you niggers to understan' dat I wa'nt bawn in de mash to be fool' by trash! I's one o' de old Blue Hen's Chickens, *I* is!" Hearing that, grown-up Henry can search childhood memories and rediscover his lost mother.

Aunt Rachel's is a vivid character which presents itself as rich in humanity, integrity, and courage. "Oh, no, Mister C_____," she concludes with mild irony, *"I hain't had no trouble, and no joy!"* The moralizing is left to our intensely aroused sympathy, admiration, and insight. The effect of revelation becomes in small what it will become, much extended, in *Adventures of Huckleberry Finn.* One thinks: if *that* is the real meaning of slavery! if *that* is what it means to be black! Twain achieves a notably realistic and democratic effect of tragic irony linked with social indignation.

The power and originality of "A True Story" recognized, it presents two interesting, inseparable problems: the dialect and the subtitle. So far as I know, there has been no satisfactory study of the passion, from De Forest through Tarkington, of the American realist for dialect and for exactness in the representation of speech. That too was a newness. The romancers generally are vulnerable to Twain's charge of offence in Cooper—that he had a tin ear for speech. More likely, since the romancer cared little for characters as such, it did not occur to him to care much about how they would talk if they were people. No Yankee artisans (no artisans anywhere) ever really talked like the lay figures in "The Artist of the Beautiful."

Yet Twain, and his editor Howells, cared intensely about the way Aunt Rachel talked. Upon accepting "A True Story" for publication Howells praised it for having "the best and reallest kind of black talk in it." Twain, pleased, volunteered to work hard on the proofs to "get the dialect as nearly right as possible." He noted his difficulty with the fact that nobody's speech is perfectly consistent and level and that to get it right he had to reproduce the actual variants. But he said, significantly, "I amend dialect stuff by talking & talking & *talking* it till it sounds right." It was his own true ear, not phonography, on which Twain relied; and he knew that the drama, concision and directness of his work depended on making the talk sound right.

Making it *seem* right was clearly the other half of the issue. The problem of "fact," the problem of the relation of facts to reality itself and to the impression, the illusion, the representation in art of reality, vexed the realist. When Twain purported to set down "A True Story Repeated Word for Word as I Heard It," there is a naive sense in which he was a simple liar. To have told "A True Story" just as it appears on the page, "Aunt Rachel" would have had to be a literary genius. Twain admitted from the start that he had rearranged the Aristotelian elements of her narrative; he probably responded to Howells's request for better "circumstantiation"; and he worked on the dialect again. How then was it "Word for Word"?

The question is much the same as that involving the discrepancies between Stephen Crane's "The Open Boat: A Tale Intended to be after the Fact . . ." and circumstances knowable from Crane's newspaper account of the experience and from external historical records. To cut swiftly through certain naive and malapropos elements of the question, the answer is that the truth, the reality toward which the realist's sensibility reached out, was human truth, the reality of personal experience. It was not, as Howells said repeatedly, the business of the realist to photograph life or map it. Vision, not sight, was the realist's business, and the metaphor which fitted what he did came from graphic art; he painted his vision of life.

Some sense of the richness and freshness of realistic opportunities in art arises from the realization that "The Beast in the Jungle" belongs to the same mode of sensibility as "A True Story." Thirty years ago there were serious, competent readers who regarded James's tale as esoteric if not opaque, but a generation of James study has accomplished something which can in part be measured by the fact that "The Beast" is today a standard anthology piece. Wholly without the traditional impedimenta, the story of May Bartram and John Marcher is a Gothic tale of personal and moral sensibilities betrayed, stifled, and petrified by romantic egotism until Marcher is left facing the horror of the utter nothingness he has made of his life and May Bartram's love. The theme is in part Hawthornian: egotism alienates, alienation leads to pride, pride to petrifaction of the heart and damnation. The heroine's name snags in one's mind—why should she share the patronym of the lime-burner in Hawthorne's tale of Ethan Brand, the man who thought he had committed the Unpardonable Sin?

The moral is also Emersonian. Evil, said Emerson, has no positive existence. It is privative, like cold, which is the absence of heat; like darkness, which is the absence of light; like death, which is the absence of life. The penalty of sin is the horror of nonbeing, the void. The literary power and the realism of James's tale stem from the exquisite tact and timing with which the sensibility of a great artist proceeds through ever-intensifying suspense to simultaneous moments of emotional release and revelation for John Marcher and the reader.

Working by "scene" and "picture" with an almost too easy mastery, James reveals to us that Marcher has trapped his soul in the romantic egotism, the Dionysian self-regard, of waiting, and watching himself wait, for a fated, unique, perhaps heroic catastrophe to top off his life. "You said," May reminds him,

> "You had had from your earliest time, as the deepest thing within you, the sense of being kept for something rare and strange, possibly prodigious and terrible, that was sooner or

later to happen to you, that you had in your bones the fore-
boding and conviction of, and that would perhaps over-
whelm you."

Subtly, gently, quietly, James lets us know that because
May loves John she takes the risk of stepping into his trap
with him, hoping that if she loves John enough she will
turn his eyes from regard of self to love and regard of
May. " 'I'll watch with you,' said May Bartram," at the
end of Section I.

Section II builds to suspense and what will be, in
retrospect, terrible irony. Marcher's concern, his almost
professional fear, raise the question of his courage. May
begins to play a role partly sibyline, partly Cassandra-
like.

" 'But doesn't the man of courage know what he's
afraid of—or *not* afraid of?' " inquires Marcher. And
then he guesses, correctly,

" 'You know something I don't. . . . You know, and
you're afraid to tell me. It's so bad that you're afraid I'll
find out.' "

But May, who is playing the game of death with her
heart, her life at stake, playing Marcher's game in the
desperate hope of getting him to turn about and take up
the game of life, can only say, " 'You'll never find out.' "

With only two characters and starkly disfurnished,
James's fiction presses on, irony by dread irony. At the
climax of Section III, learning that May is ill and might
die, Marcher feels let down at the prospect of his game's
being diminished by the loss of his spectator and is delivered up to the intolerable fear that his fate might never
strike: "He had but one desire left—that he shouldn't
have been 'sold.' " (The word, in quotation marks like a
neologism but borrowed from the lexicon of Western humor, rings with allusiveness.) In fact, of course, Marcher
has gulled himself, and Nemesis holds him firmly in

hand. At almost their last interview May tells him that truth but also that " 'The door's open,' " and " 'It's never too late.' " But as he leaves she has another prophetic word. He will not hear or see her truly, and she exclaims in pain. What has happened? he wonders: " 'What *was* to,' she said." In their last conversation she tells him, " 'You've *had* it.' " And at the very last, " 'I would live for you still—if I could. . . . But I can't!' "

The ultimate scene is one of James's achievements. Alone, baffled, a touristic ghost, Marcher wanders at length to May Bartram's grave and there meets in "the face of a fellow mortal" the shock of revelation. A man mourning at the next grave turns, unconsciously, on Marcher a face distorted by genuine grief, "the image of scarred passion." Then it appears, shockingly in this hitherto ultracivilized fiction, that the title is as organic as any of George Herbert's. All at once Marcher sees, stupefied, overwhelmed, the truth of his condition. Never having known passion, he has lived in emptiness, darkness, and cold, diminishing to the void:

> The fate he had been marked for he had met with a vengeance—he had emptied the cup to the lees; he had been the man of his time, *the* man, to whom nothing on earth was to have happened. That was the rare stroke—that was his visitation.

And now he can see:

> The escape would have been to love her; then, *then* he would have lived. *She* had lived—who could say now with what passion?—since she had loved him for himself; whereas he had never thought of her (ah how it hugely glared at him!) but in the chill of his egotism and the light of her use.

Seeing, remembering and re-seeing, knowing at last,

He saw the Jungle of his life and saw the lurking Beast;
then, while he looked, perceived it, as by a stir of the air,
rise, huge and hideous, for the leap that was to settle him.
His eyes darkened—it was close; and, instinctively turning,
in his hallucination, to avoid it, he flung himself, face
down, on the tomb.

James's brilliant last word is altogether symbolic, but
the symbol functions after the fashion of a realist. In
contrast with the butterfly of "The Artist of the Beautiful," the symbolic reference looks not outward to a general reference like Beauty (or even, in this particular
case, to a generality like Death). The horror of nothingness (his nothingness, his fate) is revealed to Marcher.
And he *has* had it. There is no going back, no escape or
refuge. But the force of James's last word in the story
presses not at all to the point that Marcher is physically
dead. Worse, it is that he has no point of reference, no
goal but the tomb, and the horror is that he must live
while he lasts in a hell of the knowledge of his self-
achieved nothingness. James's symbol, the symbol of a
realist, points inward to illuminate and reinforce the
work of art. It is left to us to generalize or moralize upon
the experience our author's sensibility has grasped and
his art made available to our ruminations.

I I I

PERHAPS THE REAL SECRET OF THE REALIST LAY IN THE
ambivalence of his sensibility with regard to romance.
He was fierce and contemptuous in rejection because he
yearned in his heart to have it. He could not slake his
thirst for the ideal because its springs had failed and
dried. Worse yet, he could not respect himself in the notion of a quest to renew the ideal in fresh creativity be-

cause idealistic belief in the midst of the intellectual crises of 1850-1890 seemed impossible. At worst it looked like mental lying, at best like mere neoromantic irresponsibility.

Therefore the realist tried first to take refuge in visible, average, common, vulgar reality. He hoped wildly that a new art, a new morality, perhaps even a new religion, could be made from a worshipful exploration of that reality. If, however, he achieved much—a critical humanism, a reforming and creative liberalism, a rich novelistic sophistication—he failed of the depths of the human heart, as Sigmund Freud and World War I would conspire to demonstrate with finality. What is more, he knew it long before either Freud or history tolled his knell. He had, in the face of his ambivalences, always known it; and after 1885 the major realistic sensibilities became conscious, in the tragic vision, of that knowledge half-hidden from themselves. The work of the realist would become increasingly psychological, increasingly symbolic. And in the fresh generation coming up to assimilate and supersede him after 1890, the realist would find a desperate newness to attack and confound him in his generational turn: the sensibility of the naturalist.

The sensibility of a naturalist may be typically represented by a sketch which the late Lars Åhnebrink picked out of Frank Norris:

> Suggestions: III, Brute
> He had been working all day in a squalid neighbourhood by the gas works and coal yards, surrounded by lifting cranes, pile drivers, dredging machines, engines of colossal, brutal strength, where all about him were immense blocks of granite, tons of pig iron; everything had been enormous, crude, had been huge in weight, tremendous in power, gigantic in size.
> By long association with such things he had become like them, huge, hard, brutal, strung with a crude, blind

strength, stupid, unreasoning. He was on his way home now, his immense hands dangling half-open at his sides; his head empty of thought. He only desired to be fed and to sleep. At a street crossing he picked up a white violet, very fresh, not yet trampled into the mud. It was a beautiful thing, redolent with the scent of the woods, suggestive of everything pretty and delicate. It was almost like a smile-made flower. It lay very light in the hollow of his immense calloused palm. In some strange way it appealed to him, and blindly he tried to acknowledge his appreciation. He looked at it stupidly, perplexed, not knowing what to do; then instinctively his hand carried it to his mouth; he ground it between his huge teeth and slowly ate it. It was the only way he knew.

Literature rests fundamentally upon anthropology in its old root sense, upon the theories of human nature held by writers and readers. Intellectually, Norris did not believe in his brute-man: as Donald Pizer has argued, Norris held philosophically melioristic, neo-idealistic convictions. Personally, Norris had never seen such a man: and he was aware of the offense he offered to the sensibility of the realist. Why, then, imagine and sketch him with such gusto? Why yearn toward the brute-man in one fiction after another? The answer is that upon Norris and all the other artists of his richly endowed generation the sensibility of the naturalist exerted a magnetic pull. Nobody was a naturalist. There really are no naturalists in American literature. Everybody born after the Civil War felt and responded after his fashion to the terrible pull of a sensibility in the grounds for which nobody finally believed.

Heuristically, it is useful if not imperative to consider the American literary generations in relation to nineteenth-century science. It opens a way to understanding the spiritual and esthetic magnetism of the new sensibility. It must at once be recognized that we are

45

talking not about *science*—the functional application of ideas to specific natural phenomena—but about *scientism*—the application of ideas derived from science to phenomena not specifically natural or properly scientific: like history, social behavior, theology, or the arts. Thus Stephen Crane was being scientistic, responding to religious implications both of theological ideas extrapolated from the sciences and to intimations of the naturalistic sensibility when he wrote:

> If I should cast off this tattered coat,
> And go free into the mighty sky;
> If I should find nothing there
> But a vast blue,
> Echoless, ignorant,—
> What then?

In certain real senses, writing that poem was an impossibility to the sensibility of the romancer: to the hearts of Hawthorne or Thoreau it was flatly inconceivable that the mighty sky should be echoless, ignorant. And Crane's poem was inconceivable to the imaginations of James or the major (one cannot be so sure of the late) Mark Twain: to the sensibility of a realist, going free into the mighty sky was boy-stuff; men stayed on earth with the earthy heart of man. Not that Crane "was" a "naturalist." Rather, the sensibility of the naturalist had become to him a vital option, an imaginably viable posture and life-style, as never before. Why? What had happened?

As Harry Hayden Clark has demonstrated, the usual simple explanations of the impact of "Darwinism"—the new scientism in general—on the ideas and sensibilities of Americans are too simple. Huxley vs. Wilberforce, Darrow vs. Bryan, science vs. fundamentalism make a line-up of dramatic (but fixed) bouts. Who, among the American writers, had been a simple fundamentalist before the Darwinian earthquake? Nobody. The problem was not nearly so much the mythologization of Genesis. It was the threatened extirpation of ideality which alienated Agassiz from his students and made Sidney Lanier cry out in pain:

> It is, somehow, a terrible reflection to me. . . . My grasses against my oaks! My ferns stabbing at the serene-shining mountain-beeches, my violets snatching the last drop of moisture from a parched and dying daisy. . . . No, in the ordinary sense of the term God is not 'good.' The suffering that goes on by His command, under His Eye, and preventable by His Hand is unspeakable. . . .

How now, Mr. Thoreau?

Exposed to the full force of a scientism which threatened to reduce the all to cosmic weather, Americans after the Civil War found themselves menaced by intellectual ghosts sprung from the graves of the Counter-Reformation. They had cold, awful Italian names: tychism, machiavellianism. If Darwinistic ideas were true and generally applicable, chaos and old night were come. The universe was reduced to a blind flow of mindless, dicey forces. Man was reduced to the merest organism fighting meaninglessly, at the mercy of chance and force, to foredoomed loss. Only a little more time in the light, a little more pleasure than pain, a little and absurd preeminence among his fellows could matter. And they too were the snares of time and force.

To a generation reared and steeped in the prime of ideality, this naturalism, the "philosophy" of Wolf Larsen, seemed a terror. Seeing its first shadows, the third and great generation of American romantics opposed it with firm rhetoric and declarations of inward assurance. "If Luther's day expand to Darwin's year,/ Shall that exclude the hope—foreclose the fear?" enquired Melville. Said Whitman, complacently:

I find I incorporate gneiss, coal, long-threaded moss,
    fruits, grains, esculent roots,
And am stucco'd with quadrupeds and birds all over,
And have distanced what is behind me for good reasons. . . .

And Thoreau, again: "I love to see that Nature is so rife with life that myriads can be afforded to be sacrificed and suffered to prey on one another. . . . The impression made on a wise man is that of universal innocence."

No doubt, a tender-minded, a neo-idealistic restoration of ideality was easiest for men whose lives through maturity had been spent in the atmosphere of ideality— easy and most necessary. Despite John Fiske, it was harder for the succeeding generation. Reared to manhood before Darwinism, they took its blow directly on the threshold of maturity. Twain's trope of learning to read the river spoke for them: romance is for boys and the innocent at large; the eye and heart of the realist know painfully reduced and bitter but valid truths.

Disillusioned, but only perhaps half, the humane sensibility of the realist was largely sheltered from the ultimate by scepticism. Not so the men who were born during the post war decade. A vital and richly creative generation, they were sheltered in youth by no indubitable idealities in American belief. Moody, Robinson, and Tarkington (1869), Norris (1870), Crane and Dreiser (1871), Frost (1875), Sherwood Anderson, Cather, London and Rölvaag (1876), they form a definite generation held together by one thing: all felt and responded to, were perhaps tempted by, though none consistently or definitively committed himself to the sensibility of a naturalist.

What was that sensibility? I think it is most easily perceived as a sense of reality and the consequences which flow from entertaining that reality seriously. It was the sense of reality a man might adopt if he willed to believe in philosophic naturalism, the last reduction of the age.

The naturalist's sense of reality stemmed from the imagination of a tough-mindedly ultimate, hard Darwinism. But it became a vision still further reduced by post-Darwinian science and scientism. Despite the pain they might cause idealists, there had been comparatively comfortable and cheery certainties in the universes offered by Comte, Herbert Spencer, or John Fiske. But now the new astronomy with its inconceivable scale and mystery began to appall: "Space ails us moderns: we are sick with space," observed Frost. Willard Gibbs with his law of entropy shook the wind out of the sails of cosmic optimists. On the other hand, the micro-universe conspired with the macro to redouble confusion. The new knowledge led not to more but less certainty, not control but mystery and defeat as the dimensions and processes of the world pushed past the limits of imagination. Even before Einstein, the possibilities of understanding, of getting an education, in human terms vanished into mist. Discovering in the work of the Curies the existence of what would become the world of electronic physics, Henry Adams found defeat at the end of his quest. "Radium denied its God," he learned, and "man had translated himself into a new universe which had no common scale of measurement with the old."

Thus was the realist's sensibility discredited, rendered unavailable to a naturalistic sensibility as the sensibility of the romancer had been lost upon realists. The fascinating upshot was that fictionally the naturalist tended to become a new romancer in dealing with character. Except that where the romancer was a superrealist the naturalist became an infrarealist. Losing his belief in the importance of persons, the naturalist was tempted to lose interest in his characters as people and begin to deal with them as symbolic tracers—chips on the stream to tell us how the great forces flow.

Not an expression of a philosophy so much as a response to the atmosphere—the climate of opinion around him—the sensibility of the naturalist, like those of his predecessors, fastened on the problem of appearance and reality. Indignantly, with abhorrence but with a sincerity somehow compulsive, the new sensibility took to be supremely real all that is sordid, squalid, dirty, slimy, repulsive, brutal, and pathetic in man and nature. Against this reality it poised everything ideal, generous, value-laden, clean, respectable, or gentle as sorry appearances, lying illusions, "the genteel tradition." His new vision brought with it serious consequences. To it the past seemed contemptible, a bucket of ashes, the residue of old dreams, old lies, old losses. It could feel only indignation toward the present (whose ideals were false, its realities vicious) or indifference or pity. It could not believe in the usefulness of taking thought or the sense in caring. It projected the contempt of Santayana, the fury of Lewis or early Brooks, the baffled compassion of Anderson, Fitzgerald, or O'Neill.

The perhaps most notable product of the naturalist's sensibility sounded like a contradiction in terms and became a literary form characterized by the effects of split sensibility and absurdity. A hard-nosed tragedy of self-pity, it brooded because man dreamed that he was made a spiritual being, but a little lower than the angels: how pitiful that it is false! Man dreamed that he was human, different from the brutes, that man's fate and values matter: how strange, how pitiful that it is false! That ignoble tragic vision, with its portion of *saeva indignatio,* constituted the motive force for a negative naturalism in fiction.

A positive naturalism might have risen from a fictional vision showing the great forces at work. Frank Norris was tempted to such a portrayal in his project for a great trilogy upon wheat, *The Octopus, The Pit,* and *The Wolf,* showing how wheat is actually a force which controls man. The farmer thinks he sows the wheat for profit; but wheat sows the farmer, or produces farmers who must sow it. And as wheat enters the stream of commerce of the world it feeds the nations or starves the nations; and the railroad men and speculators, the merchants and the statesmen who think they control the wheat are in fact fated by its forces natural and social. Any effort to make steady sense of Theodore Dreiser is difficult. He possessed one of the intellectually most unstable minds that ever wrote fiction. But one of the Dreisers was an author who felt deeply the pathos, the pity of the fact that weak, common human beings could be trapped in their illusions by vast forces and wiped out, as in *An American Tragedy* or *Sister Carrie.*

Nevertheless, it is probably true that there are not finally any naturalists. I am not aware of a work of fiction which will stand adequately and consistently for the naturalistic sensibility. There was only a sensibility to be fragmentarily, inconsistently, or occasionally expressed. Nobody, at least in American literature, could bear to be its thoroughgoing exponent. Everybody found some way to turn the sensibility aside, to compromise, to deny it. I have argued elsewhere that Stephen Crane only entertained, never espoused it and that "The Open Boat" is the test case. Robinson and Frost fought naturalism all their lives, clear evidence of its magnetism. Norris, Jack London, and Dreiser talked brave naturalism but never uncompromisingly wrote it. Beneath and around their commitments were governing, antinaturalistic loyalties to man. The writers took refuge in reform, humanitarianism, socialism. Above all, in the end they turned humane. London even waxed anthropomorphic, nature-faking, about wolves.

Perhaps the one who most nearly bore the naturalist's agony was Robinson Jeffers, the great California poet who called his philosophy "Inhumanism." A first-rate expression of his feel for the sensibility comes in the poem "Margrave," where he undercut the contradictions of a naturalistic tragedy by providing a narrative commentator to combat openly the absurdities of indignation and self-pity felt by the poem's protagonists. Such a commentary as the following seems to me to come as close to a full, consistent naturalism as any writing I know:

> The learned astronomer
> Analyzing the light of most remote star-swirls
> Has found them—or a trick of distance deludes his prism—
> All at incredible speeds fleeing outward from ours. . . .
>
> So, I thought, the rumor
> Of human consciousness had gone abroad in the world,
> The sane uninfected far-outer universes
> Flee it in a panic of escape. . . .
>
> I believe this hurt will be healed
> Some age of time after mankind has died,
> Then the sun will say, "What ailed me a moment?" and resume
> The old soulless triumph; . . .
>
> But who is our judge? It is likely the enormous
> Beauty of the world requires for completion our ghostly increment,
> It has to dream, and dream badly, a moment of its night.

There is argument as to whether Jeffers was a naturalist. If not, I do not know who was, certainly nobody more compromising. I do not know where to find the naturalist's sensibility better registered, better expressed; and the sensibility is easier to find in literature than the "ism."

3 / The Batrachomyomachia

and American Fiction

Like other Renaissance men, the earliest American literati felt a responsibility to the great tradition of the epic; and, especially in New England, they felt somewhat equal to their duty. No doubt that was the idea behind such titles as *The Tenth Muse Lately Sprung up in America* and *Magnalia Christi Americana*. The dutiful impulse, however, never rose higher in performance than *The Triumph of Infidelity* or *The Columbiad*, of which the best one can say is that at the same time epics no better were being published in Europe. Americans proved to be not up to the epic: mock-heroic was more their style. Fortunately, they had also a tradition there to fall back upon. Not *Paradise Lost* but *Hudibras*, not *The Iliad* but *The Batrachomyomachia*, not epic but mock-epic govern the traditions of American fiction.

There is almost nothing to say about the classical model, the text, its authorship, its date. It comes to us with that apparently autochthonous inevitability with which ignorance shrouds the classics. To put it in a nutshell, as surely as Alexander the Great pillowed his mad, imperial head upon Homer, nature demanded a *Batrachomyomachia*. Depending on one's theory of the survival and transmission of classical literature, the mock-epic of the war between the frogs and the mice proved to be either the best of burlesque parodies of Homer or the luckiest. At any rate, it survives to stand beside *Lysistrata* and assure us that men in classical antiquity were neither simple nor foolish. They knew a bad thing when they saw it. They reacted against too much of a good thing. They understood the uses of wit, parody, burlesque, and travesty to subvert established pomposity and authorized egomania.

There is no need to recapitulate the definitive work of Richmond P. Bond and illustrate again the ambivalences of neoclassical England's worship of the epic beside its passion for the mock-heroic. What I must hasten to recall is that eighteenth-century Americans, with their Provincial culture centered on London, fell heirs to the same ambivalence. In ways increasingly American, they too felt the reaction against the European wars of sectarian carnage and read Cervantes. They too traced the English line of mock-heroic sentiment through Hudibras Butler, Swift, Pope, Smollett, and Sterne. But there came in the last third of the century to be a distinctively American response to the mock-heroic impulse.

I

FOR REASONS OBVIOUS ENOUGH, WE FORGET THAT OUR revered Founding Fathers deliberately chose odium when they chose rebellion. It was inevitably and overwhelmingly regarded in Europe as contemptible. Certain American counter-gestures became important. It was not merely the political treason: "Gentlemen, we must hang together or we shall hang separately," Franklin said. Rebellion offended civilized sensibilities. The rebel threw in his lot with the vulgar, the dirty, mean, low rabble. It was despicable as well as impious to trample Cross and Crown in the mire.

The intelligent despised have, however, a lovely weapon in parody. As Freneau observed anent his rival, the Royalist printer James Rivington,

The *Crown* is so worn of your master the despot,
That I hardly know which 'tis (a crown or a piss-pot)

Thus Hopkinson slanted "The Battle of the Kegs"; and Trumbull went straight to the batrachomyomachian line in subverting the valor of Tories. Here is Trumbull's M'Fingal in mock-heroic combat:

Swift turn'd M'Fingal at the view,
And call'd to aid th' attendant crew,
In vain; the Tories all had run,
When scarce the fight was well begun;
Their setting wigs he saw decreas'd
Far in th' horizon tow'rd the west.
Amazed he view'd the shameful sight,
And saw no refuge, but in flight:
But age unwieldy check'd his pace,
Though fear had wing'd his flying race;
For not a trifling prize at stake;
No less than great M'Fingal's back.
With legs and arms he work'd his course,
Like rider that outgoes his horse,
And labor'd hard to get away, as
Old Satan struggling on through chaos;
'Till looking back, he spied in rear
The spade-arm'd chief advanced too near:
Then stopp'd and seized a stone, that lay
An ancient landmark near the way;
Nor shall we as old bards have done,
Affirm it weigh'd an hundred ton;
But such a stone, as at a shift
A modern might suffice to lift,
Since men, to credit their enigmas,
Are dwindled down to dwarfs and pigmies,

And giants exiled with their cronies
To Brobdingnags and Patagonias.
But while our Hero turn'd him round,
And tugg'd to raise it from the ground,
The fatal spade discharged a blow
Tremendous on his rear below:
His bent knee fail'd, and void of strength
Stretch'd on the ground his manly length.
Like ancient oak o'erturn'd, he lay,
Or tower to tempests fall'n a prey,
Or mountain sunk with all his pines,
Or flow'r the plow to dust consigns,
And more things else—but all men know 'em,
If slightly versed in epic poem.

But nothing has ever been simple or unified in American life and literature. We should all paste in our hats Merle Curti's dictum. After a lifetime of studying the history of the mind in our country, he felt authorized to make one ironic generalization: it always displays unity in diversity, and diversity in unity. The Revolution had not ended before Americans began to quarrel about domestic heroes. One might write a history of American literature from 1780 to 1820 around the question, who was the American Anti-hero? The range of candidates spanned a wide, fateful spectrum: the traditional aristocrat, the pseudo-aristocrat; the upstart commoner, the pseudo-commoner; the dead-pan humorist. Issues became thoroughly scrambled during the evolutionary Federalist-Republican political and intellectual wars. The result became a series of shifting multivalences in American thought. But the mock-heroic attitude and American expertise in the use of mock-heroic techniques became permanently established.

One sees this in the obsessive writings of such Federalist figures as Thomas Green Fessenden. And the "aristocrats" were inventively attacked in such a deadpan rejoinder as Philip Freneau's evasion of the Alien and Sedition Act by posing as Robert Slender, O.S.M. The honorific letters were mock-innocently adapted from Burke and Alexander Hamilton. "O.S.M.," said Slender proudly, was an Order to which he felt natively entitled. It meant, "One of the Swinish Multitude."

The precarious balance and halting gait of what might be called the basic American mock-heroic is nowhere better exemplified than in Hugh Henry Brackenridge's *Modern Chivalry*. I feel moved to protest against the fashion established by Richard Chase of beginning the history of American fiction with Charles Brockden Brown. There are certain tendentious advantages to so commencing; but that is part of the objection. Brackenridge was earlier, he was more substantial, and he was in virtually everything the opposite of Brown. If Brown may be said to lead toward the American romance, Brackenridge leads toward the novel. Brackenridge worked in the traditions of Cervantes, *Hudibras,* Swift, and Smollett. The least one can say, according with Curti, is that the American novel and its tradition began in plurality, ambivalence, even conflict.

And a work essential to proper historical consideration but wrongly, as I think, left out of modern histories of American fiction, is Washington Irving's *Knickerbocker History of New York.* For the shifts and mixtures of modes, forms, ideas, and sensibilities in *Modern Chivalry* there was precedent and authority in Rabelais, Cervantes, Fielding, and Sterne. And just so for the *Knickerbocker History.* As history that huge fiction was a baggy put-on. Immediate social and political intention in the American tradition gave a particular edge to Diedrich Knickerbocker's version of *The Batrachomyomachia.* To illustrate, Book VI brings Peter Stuyvesant and the Dutch to assault Jan Risingh and the Swedes:

The immortal deities, who whilome had seen service at the affair of Troy—now mounted their feather-bed clouds, and sailed over the plain, or mingled among the combatants in different disguises, all itching to have a finger in the pie. Jupiter sent off his thunderbolt to a noted coppersmiths, to have it furbished up for the direful occasion. Venus, swore by her chastity she'd patronize the Swedes, and in semblance of a blear eyed trull, paraded the battlements of Fort Christina, accompanied by Diana, as a serjeant's widow, of cracked reputation—The noted bully Mars, stuck two horse pistols into his belt, shouldered a rusty firelock, and gallantly swaggered at their elbow, as a drunken corporal—while Apollo trudged in their rear, as a bandy-legged fifer, playing most villainously out of tune.

At length, of course, conventional necessity brings the two generals to single combat:

No sooner did these two rival heroes come face to face, than they each made a prodigious start of fifty feet, (flemish measure) such as is made by your most experienced stage champions. Then did they regard each other for a moment, with bitter aspect, like two furious ram cats, on the very point of a clapper clawing. Then did they throw themselves in one attitude, then in another, striking their swords on the ground, first on the right side, then on the left, at last at it they went, like five hundred houses on fire! Words cannot tell the prodigies of strength and valour, displayed in this direful encounter—an encounter, compared to which the far famed battles of Ajax with Hector, of Eneas with Turnus, Orlando with Rodomont, Guy of Warwick with Colbrand the Dane, or of that renowned Welsh Knight Sir Owen of the mountains with the giant Guylon, were all gentle sports and holliday recreations. . . . the stout Risingh collecting all his forces, aimed a mighty blow, full at the hero's crest. In vain did his fierce little cocked hat oppose its course; the biting steel clove through the stubborn ram beaver, and would infallibly have cracked his gallant crown, but that the scull was of such adamantine hardness that the brittle weapon shivered into five and twenty pieces, shedding a thousand sparks, like beams of glory, round his grizly visage.

   Stunned with the blow the valiant Peter reeled, turned up his eyes and beheld fifty thousand suns, besides moons and stars, dancing Scotch reels about the firmament—at length, missing his footing, by reason of his wooden leg, down he came, on his seat of honour, with a crash that shook the surrounding hills, and would infallibly have wracked his anatomical system, had he not been received into a cushion softer than velvet, which providence, or Minerva, or St. Nicholas, or some kindly cow, had benevolently prepared for his reception.

At this rate, the "fact" of Stuyvesant's "victory" attains a significance wholly ridiculous. What is now significant to literary understanding is that this mockery attached to no mere episode in the *Knickerbocker History*. As fiction it maintained a point of view steadily oblique, reductive, and subversive. Yet its author was to become the first unquestionably romantic American artist. As a romantic, he would also remain what he was from the first, an able, inveterate ironist. Reared a Federalist and neoclassicist, Irving may be said to have been disillusioned into becoming Jacksonian and romantic. The first American romantic commenced disillusioned, possessed of multiple vision, and ironic. And, textbook wishfulness to the contrary notwithstanding, of what major American romantic author may the same not be said? I think there is none.

I I

THE MEANING OF ALL THIS TO AN UNDERSTANDING OF American fiction is our present question, and to face it more squarely one must in a sense make another beginning. The cases crucial to our discussion must be Cooper and Hawthorne. To both of them a distinction brought down from the generations immediately past was important. Both proposed to understand the creation of fiction by looking to a distinction between "the novel" and "the romance." A simple way to define "the romance" is to say that it is the kind of fiction a romantic would write. Then when you know what kind of romantic you are dealing with you can define his kind of romance. That method has its uses, but not here. It will be better to look to the tradition.

In the standard discussion, Clara Reeve's *The Progress of Romance,* 1785, had proposed this set of definitions:

> The Romance is an heroic fable, which treats of fabulous persons and things.—The Novel is a picture of real life and manners, and of the times in which it is written. The Romance in lofty and elevated language, describes what never happened nor is likely to happen.—The Novel gives a familiar relation of such things, as pass every day before our eyes, . . . in so easy and natural a manner, . . . as to deceive us into a persuasion (at least while we are reading) that all is real. . . .

Ignoring for the moment Platonic considerations, to the American Democrat (as Cooper, in his fashion anticipating Whitman, called him) the problem of fiction presented itself as a problem in tensions between epic-romantic-aristocratic elevation and batrachomyomachian-democratic reduction for the sake of common reality and republican virtue. The tension comes out strikingly in Cooper, who could never decide whether he was to be a stern republican censor or a constructive romancer. In one stance he was an antiromantic censor and if not a novelist then a mock-heroic satirist. This accounts for *The Crater, The Monikins,* such double-barreled works as *Homeward Bound* and *Home As Found,* or *Miles Wal-*

lingford and *Afloat and Ashore,* and for the Anti-Rent trilogy. It also accounts for certain of the instabilities Mark Twain pointed out in characterizations of Cooper's Leatherstocking and Indians. Cooper the constructive romancer idealized them; Cooper the censor, who was his own kind of socialist realist, rather disapproved of and mocked them. Again, the early American novelist, looking to a nascent tradition, found multiplicity.

A good illustration of such multiplicity is provided by an implicit exchange between Hawthorne and William Gilmore Simms. With prime faith in Sir Walter Scott, Simms wrote in his "Advertisement" to *The Yemassee,* 1835:

> The question briefly is, what are the standards of the modern romance—what is the modern romance itself? The reply is instant. Modern romance is the substitute which the people of to-day offer for the ancient epic. Its standards are the same. . . .
>
> The modern romance is a poem in every sense of the word. It is only with those who insist upon poetry as rhyme, and rhyme as poetry, that the identity fails to be perceptible. Its standards are precisely those of the epic.

Obviously there was much said and more implied by Simms with which Hawthorne the historical romancer might gladly have agreed. But for Hawthorne the sceptic, the democrat, the idealist, there were difficulties in the proposal that to elevate historical fact toward the heroic boundaries of credibility would create viable romance and modern epic. Though one doubts that Simms followed *The Salem Gazette,* Hawthorne replied to him in an obscure account of *Views and Reviews.* Said Hawthorne:

> . . . we cannot help feeling that the real treasures of his subject have escaped the author's notice. The themes sug-

gested by him, viewed as he views them, would produce nothing but historical novels, cast in the same worn out mould that has been in use these thirty years, and which it is time to break up and fling away. To be the prophet of Art requires almost as high a gift as to be a fulfiller of the prophecy. Mr. Simms has not this gift; he possesses nothing of the magic touch that should cause new intellectual and moral shapes to spring up in the reader's mind, peopling with varied life what had hitherto been a barren waste.

Hawthorne's esthetic was Platonic if not transcendental; and he was getting at the point, of which Emerson and Whitman made much, that perhaps the one way to join the epic-romantic with the democratic-vulgar was to unite them in a sort of Hegelian triad. If there be truth in the doctrine of correspondence, and natural facts *are* symbols of spiritual facts, then common men and their experience may become more heroic than Homer or Milton supposed. It was a heady thought. Emerson made fine poems out of his experience of converting doubts into flashes of revelation, but he attempted nothing even remotely epic. Roy Harvey Pearce is, I think, definitive on Whitman's distance from the epic (supposing Walt ever intended anything of the sort).

But Hawthorne in a sense copped out. He found indeed "the magic touch that should cause new intellectual and moral shapes to spring up in the reader's mind"; but he managed to eat his transcendental cake and keep his democratic doubts. As Terence Martin has explained, Hawthorne's invention of "the neutral ground" for fiction was neither of this world nor out of it, elevated but not heroic, both romantic and novelistic. Above all, Hawthorne's position was pluralistic, even shifty. He was prepared at any moment to betray his reader and deprecate himself. Without sympathizing, one can understand Henry James's exasperation.

I I I

To BEGIN AGAIN FOR THE LAST TIME, THE ASSERTIONS I have been making have revisionist implications for American literary history. I suppose the most interesting presumptive question in the current study of American literature is whether a thesis of Matthiessen as developed by such major heirs as Richard Chase, Charles Feidelson, and R.W.B. Lewis is exclusively correct: is it of the nature of the American imagination that it yearns, perhaps helplessly, for the fulfillments of Romance, the romantic? Are there no other fundamental considerations? Unless we start from this thesis, must we go wrong?

Such appears to be the theme of that impressive but elusive book, *The American Novel and Its Tradition*. A corollary of its thesis—that a necessary impulse of the American poet drives him toward the native epic—became a major principle of relevance in *The Continuity of American Poetry*. And an obvious deduction from Chase and Pearce would be that the aim of the American romance must also be the epic. Chase quoted Simms, glancingly, to that effect. Some such idea seems to have become a ruling cliché in the criticism of traditional American fiction. It will not come as a surprise when I say that I wish to challenge the whole set of propositions.

The intellectual experience of the first half of the current century reversed certain late nineteenth-century faiths and restored the credibility of many romantic concerns and beliefs. This restoration led critics to the conviction that we must insist upon discovering and emphasizing *our* romanticisms as we read the literature of the past. It might not be too much to say that such an insistence has in substantial degree predetermined certain qualities of the literature being written in our own time. Yet I must confess to feeling troubled by two aspects of such notions. Treating the past as if it were not to be valued *except* in terms of the present, we are tempted to falsify the past with every wind of intellectual fashion that blows. Difficult, impossible though it may be to know the past in its pastness as it was, we owe the past and ourselves more stability than that. Certainly we owe to literary documents the mere confrontation of their fulness, not just convenient fragments. Further, given our failures, our state of eternal crisis, the blinding speed of change, it might behoove us to seek as well as we can to find the past on its terms and see what it has to teach us.

Therefore, while the power of the romance-epic impulse is too strong to be overlooked or denied in studying the life of the American mind, it seems strange to the point of illegitimacy to ignore the power of counterimpulses toward the common, democratic, mock-heroic, and novelistic. Observation of the tensions (often creative) between the two traditions might be rewarding; they might account for the esthetic force of certain works in spite of the oft-lamented failure of the heroic imagination in American literature. I plead, in short, for a new pluralism in American literary criticism and history. In the remainder of this chapter I shall try to suggest certain rewards of adding batrachomyomachian considerations to our understanding.

The values of *The Batrachomyomachia* and its descendants are both formal and moral. Its art is the art of sinking, of bathos, of building up to an awful let-down. When we are weary of high sentence, high seriousness, pomp, circumstance, spilled brains, guts, and gore, superhuman act and attitude, we turn with relish and relief to burlesque. One is then reminded that the heroic suffers from diseases not only of rhetoric and the imagination but also of the heart. Frogs and mice declaiming and pretending to act Homeric are ridiculous. But if they, why not we—even our generals or statesmen or champions? The batrachomyomachian cure for the superhuman ego is to chop it off at the knees and cut it down to a human, preferably humane, level. Hawthorne certainly applied some such technique to the climax of *The House of the Seven Gables,* which is why he taunts dead Judge Pyncheon, sitting there before the mocking portrait, his meaningless watch in his hand, dead of drinking the blood of his hereditary curse. Other crucial characters in Hawthorne seem to stand in like case: Ethan Brand and Chillingworth, perhaps Dimmesdale, probably young Goodman Brown.

Considering Hawthorne leads at once to Melville, and one need only recall the mock-heroic ingredients among the foundational ambivalences of *Moby-Dick.* We have begun, fortunately, to abandon the notion that *Moby-Dick* is a great, pure work of heroic dimensions— either an epic with the whale as hero or a tragedy centered upon Ahab. I feel almost ready to hazard the contention that every aspect of tragic or heroic "magnitude" in the book has been carefully undercut. There can be no doubt that Melville made epic borrowings, particularly from Milton. But did he borrow for epical or for mock-heroic ends? or for *both* ends? His general precedents, after all, were the books of Rabelais, Cervantes, Browne, and Sterne—and at home those of Brackenridge and Irving. And, reader, were not these all great, mixed, bathetic monsters?

In Mark Twain's *Adventures of Huckleberry Finn* certain mock-heroic attitudes have always been obvious. Twain framed his novel in treatments of boy-life and its irresponsible romanticisms, making so much mock-heroic hay of them that there has been a somewhat ill-considered outcry against their extension to the end-frame. What has perhaps not been sufficiently noticed is the pervasiveness of mock-heroic undercutting through-out the book's main action, the descent down the river. I find it hard to swallow the notion that the main action is a romance—perhaps a frontier epic, a pastoral idyll, or a mythic Initiation replete with rites of passage—when the constituent actions are so consistently batrachomyoma-chian. Consider Huck and Jim on the wrecked steamboat *Sir Walter Scott*, or the Grangerford-Sheperdson feud, or the Duke and the Dauphin in all their works, or Colonel Sherburn on the subject of Arkansas.

Boy-chivalry is silly enough; but man-chivalry is stupid, mendacious, and vicious to boot. As Twain told Howells, he couldn't bear to carry Tom Sawyer through to manhood.

I suspect that the key to Twain's double line of mock-heroic attack lies in the famous passage about learning to read the river in "Old Times on the Mississippi." When you learn a true use of your eyes, all the romantic illusions of beauty and safety dissolve away: what remains is a true vision of menaces to be navigated the best you can. Romantic egotism in adults is "Sir Walter Scottism," not only silly but vicious: dangerous to the bearer of the disease, to his victims, and to civilization.

There is space to deal perhaps with the one last work which nobody considering the epic and the American novel dare leave out. One American novelist declared that he believed in reviving the epic, that he was going to write an epic trilogy; and he survived to get two volumes done. That was of course Frank Norris. He proposed to Howells in 1899 to write "a big Epic trilogy . . . that at the same time would be modern and distinctly American" about Wheat, "this huge, Niagara of wheat rolling from West to East." There is a kind of general agreement among critics that the second volume, *The Pit,* won't do, which leaves us to consider *The Octopus,* certainly an impressive, intriguing novel still rather inscrutable to criticism.

The notion that one might be able to explicate *The Octopus* by coming at it from an epical angle, so to speak, is strengthened by knowing that Norris declared himself loudly in favor of the American epic. Every other nation had its epic, Norris lamented, "But the American epic, just as heroic, just as elemental, just as important and as picturesque will fade into history" uncelebrated. So far, apparently, so good. Unfortunately, Norris did not hold up. It turns out that in his essay "A Neglected Epic" Norris was dashing off hasty hack-work. His neglected American epic hero turns out all too actually to be the Western pioneer libeled in pulp fiction, caricatured in horse opera. Said Norris, unconsciously demanding *The Virginian:*

> The great figure of our neglected epic, the Hector of our ignored Iliad, is not, as the dime novels would have us believe, a lawbreaker, but a lawmaker; a fighter, it is true, as is always the case with epic figures, but a fighter for peace, a calm, grave, strong man who hated the lawbreaker as the hound hates the wolf.
>
> He did not lounge in barrooms; he did not cheat at cards; he did not drink himself to maudlin fury; he did not "shoot at the drop of the hat." But he loved his horse, he loved his friend, he was kind to little children. . . .

Actually, the ostensibly epic qualities of *The Octopus* seem just about equally embarrassing. Not even Donald Pizer, Norris's ablest illuminator, undertakes to defend or even much explore them. Norris's trouble was that his heroic sense apprehended not heroic men or deeds (on the contrary) but heroic Force, supreme Life-Force, of which the Wheat served as emblem and agent. He glimpsed the Force as vaguely heroic but could of course imagine for it neither character nor plot. In net effect, human actualities in *The Octopus* drop into bathos (worst of all, unintentional bathos). Emerson had said, maliciously,

> The god who made New Hampshire
> Taunted the lofty land with little men.

In the epic sense, *The Octopus* obtained the same effect in spite of Frank Norris.

Finally, however, epic failure is not so destructive of *The Octopus* as might be supposed. The batrachomyomachian moral effect at which Emerson aimed consorts easily with a Hebraic religious awe: "What is man that thou art mindful of him?" And as Pizer's explanation of Norris's ideas in consonance with the thought of Joseph Le Conte has shown us, reverence for the Life-Force informed *The Octopus*. It is also true that a sense of man's diminishment in the face of Nature was and would remain an ingredient basic to the sensibility of naturalism. The results remain, however, quite destructive of the notion of epic quality in *The Octopus*. It might be remarked that the same holds for such other miscalled epic novelists of our century as Dos Passos.

To conclude I can do no better than quote Thomas Greene, an incomparably superior student of epic:

> As man's pride has been increasingly humbled since the seventeenth century, it has taken less assertive form. The imagination has responded . . . by producing the novel, which turns from awe to analysis, from heaven and hell to the subtly and minutely human.

The nineteenth century, he continues, saw the epic

> . . . still further displaced from the mainstream of serious literature, forced to risk either bombast or triviality. And the heroes of the twentieth century are hemmed in by the intractable. These developments are scarcely subject to cavil. . . .

Not only developments of the more modern mind away from the aristocratic grounds for epic, the personal, democratic, and humane have been aspects of the American mind from its inception. *That* in general terms is why our literature, and especially our fiction, has been poor in epic but rich in mock-epic qualities.

4 / Native Sources

IN RETROSPECT, EVEN HOWELLS FELT LESS THAN CONCLU-
sive about where realism came from. Apparently it
was in personal conversation that he told Arthur Hobson
Quinn that as a novelist he had felt "authorized rather
than inspired" by the French. But of the American realists he told the great audience gathered to celebrate his
seventy-fifth birthday, "I would fain help to have it
remembered that we studied from the French masters,
the continental masters. . . ." He might, of course, have
been both consistent and right, but a certain confusion
suggests itself.

If, on the other hand, Howells actually did feel confused about the sources of American realism, his feeling
was warranted. If, as folk-say goes, you are not confused,
you don't understand the situation. The sources were immensely complex. There was a great contemporaneous
realistic movement, European rather than British, which
deeply influenced the Americans. Those long walks
given to endless talk about the novel which Henry James
took with Howells in Cambridge during the late 1860's
often concerned "the continental masters." Still, there is
something richly suggestive in the distinction between

"authorized" and "inspired." It suggests in Howells's case what could in fact be demonstrated: that he had begun to move toward realism as a teen-aged printer smuggling fiction into the family newspaper, or as a reporter in Columbus, Ohio, or as a consul in Venice—long years before he began to walk with Henry James.

One way to grasp a seldom-considered aspect of the question is to grant the massive, inevitable effect of Europe and ask what so prepared Americans to receive it? Without agitating the British side of the issue, why were Americans so much readier for realism? Were there local, "native" sources of realism and, if so, what were they?

I

To anyone familiar with American literary and cultural history certain answers suggest themselves at once. For one thing, some of the popular romanticisms which have dominated our culture since it began have always teetered on the edge of metamorphizing into realism. And certain whole-hearted romantics occasionally let themselves slip over the edge. *Satanstoe,* "Hamatreya," Thoreau knowing beans, Hosea Biglow talking, old Ishmael reflecting on his youthful self, "Come Up From the Fields Father," and the preface to "Among the IIills" are all the realistic creations of romantic imaginations. The romanticisms of the homely, the low, the familiar lent themselves readily to reductive translation. So did the impulses to nativism, local color, and the regional.

Romanticism reacting against itself, guilty about its rejections of the dominant American practicality, its intuitive pragmatism, its established philosophy of common sense, could make Hawthorne yearn to be Trollope, rack Whittier with laughter at his temptation to act Byronic, turn Irving, Holmes, and Bret Harte toward romantic irony and self-parody. Bohemianism, as in Henry Clapp and his fleeting school, with its neo-Byronic hatred of sentimentality and gentility, looked toward realism. And American democratic ideals ("God must have loved the common people: He made so many of them") adored the simple, separate person and learned to be specific and exact in attacking the crimes of aristocracy and autocracy against the common man. Obviously the print-shop and its newspaper, the poor boy's college, taught many a poor but bright boy (like Clemens and Howells) how to look from folly to fact. Romanticism for common Americans often became, in spite of itself, a school of irony. And while irony may not lead to revolt, or, having so led, may not let one rest in realism, it has, from Nathaniel Ward to Louis Auchincloss, often pointed a realistic way.

But there were two dominant cultural modes in mid-nineteenth-century America in which the literary realists of the latter century were schooled. All had some sort of instruction in them. For Howells, Clemens, and James, the major figures, they were variously but centrally decisive. Though superficially different, they were at root significantly connected. They were the mode of "American," or "frontier," humor and the mode of travel writing.

I I

WHAT MOST DEEPLY CONNECTED TRAVEL LITERATURE to frontier humor and both to realism was the sense of cultural relativity in which all three were grounded. Class relations and conflict, whether from gentry to commoner, rich man to poor, European traveler to American, dandy to squatter, Easterner to frontiersman, savant to illiterate, lay at the heart of a humor which became "Western" because its practitioners seemed disadvantaged. Humor was a weapon for turning the tables, and it began (of course) in the earliest "West," the beach-head frontier of the Atlantic tidewaters.

Consciously or not, Governor John Winthrop recorded a fine bit of frontier humor from as early as 1645. The universal frontier shortage of labor having befallen theocratic Massachusetts, there came a parting of the ways between "one of Rowley and his servant":

> The master, being forced to sell a pair of his oxen to pay his servant his wages, told his servant he could keep him no longer, not knowing how to pay him the next year. The servant answered, he would serve him for more of his cattle. But how shall I do (saith the master) when all my cattle are gone? The servant replied, you shall then serve me, and so you may have your cattle again.

Whether she quite understood or told the tale out of malice, the Boston traveler Sarah Kemble Knight collected a gem of purest water in darkest Connecticut in 1704. Probably an innocent handler of stolen goods, an Indian was charged with stealing a hogshead and hustled off to confront the magistrate. Since the majesty of the law was harvesting pumpkins in his field, court was convened at once with the magistrate and his associate presiding upon a bench constructed from the crop. "Which being finished," wrote Madame Knight,

> down seatts their Worships, and the Malefactor call'd, and by the Senior Justice Interrogated after the following manner. You Indian why did You steal from this man. You sho'dn't do so—it's a Grandy wicked thing to steal. Hol't Hol't, cryes Justice Junr. Brother, You speak negro to him. I'le ask him. You sirrah, why did you steal this man's Hoggshead. Hoggshead? (replys the Indian) me no stomany. No? says his Worship; and pulling off his hatt,

Patted his own head with his hand, sais, Tatapa—You, Tatapa—you; all one this. Hoggshead all one this. Hah! says Netop, now me stomany that. Whereupon the Company fell into a great fitt of Laughter, even to Roreing, Silence is commanded, but to no effect: for they continued perfectly Shouting. Nay, says his worship, in an angry tone, if it be so, *take mee off the Bench.*

Artistically the yarners stiffly recorded by antique Bostonians were a long way from Harris, Hooper, and Clemens. But they were already in the vein. Twain's first published piece, "The Dandy Frightening the Squatter," meant in large the same thing, social leveling, as the story Howells treasured from his youth in the print-shop about the schoolmarm surprised out back in the bushes who kept her poise for quite a while as she explained that she had just come out to pick a few blackberries for tea —hee-hee-hee-hee!

Frontier humor was an offensive-defensive weapon against cultural superiority, social snobbery, and personal contempt. It worked well against dukes and dudes and dandies, against Horace Greeley and Mrs. Trollope and Matthew Arnold. Especially it protected against missionaries, teachers, preachers, uplifting ladies, and visitors planning to write books. It evened things up with Europe, the East, urbanism, and civilization on the make. And its method, always and from every angle, was to undercut elevation and puncture pomposity. "I've been lingerin by the Tomb of the lamented Shakspeare," wrote Artemus Ward from tourist-haunted Stratford-on-Avon, "It is a success."

As a leveling device, humor assumed that invidious comparisons existed. It set out to puncture, deflate, undermine, and undercut. Its serious business, aside from entertainment, was reduction. Therein lay its perfect parallel with negative realism as an intellectual revolt against romantic superhumanism and as a literary attack upon romantic elevation. An American humorist, trained to the joy of deflating every variety of pretence and afflatus, rich in the techniques of a folk art tirelessly exercised by oral and journalistic experts on every village square, was potentially a formidable realist.

I I I

WHAT MORE NATURAL PATH FOR THE AMERICAN HUmorist hot on the spoor of romantic idiocy than to come with secure delight upon the American pilgrimizing toward Europe, to seize upon the innocents abroad? But before Twain did that, Howells had stumbled upon a realer Venice behind the gaudy scrims of Byron and Ruskin. The innocent abroad might be an inspired idiot; but he might be a child of penetrating eye as well. The realists' discovery of the uses of travel writing set them on the way to transcending satire and deflation, to creating a new sort of American literature, toward a positive realism.

One almost sure path to fame and affluence in the romantic era had been to go to some exotic place and give it a glamorous write-up. Everybody tried it: Irving, Cooper, Longfellow, Hawthorne, Melville. George W. Curtis and Bayard Taylor founded careers on traveling and telling about it. Emerson's only book is *English Traits;* the essential point of view in *Walden* looks out from the announcement, "I have travelled much in Concord."

Whittier put a shrewd finger on the initial, naive aim of the genre in a review of Taylor's "Forty-niner" book, *Eldorado.* "Blessings on the man who invented books of travel for the benefit of home idlers!" wrote the invalid:

When the cark and care of daily life and homely duties, and the wearing routine of sight and sound, oppress us, what a comfort and refreshing is it to open the charmed pages of the traveller! Our narrow, monotonous horizon breaks away all about us; five minutes suffice to take us quite out of the commonplace and familiar regions of our experience. . . . We look into the happiness of travelling through the eyes of others, and for the miseries of it, we enjoy *them* exceedingly. Very cool and comfortable are we while reading the poor author's account of his mishaps, hairbreadth escapes, hunger, cold, and nakedness. . . . Let him meet with what he will—robbers, cannibals, jungle-tigers, and rattlesnakes, the more the better—since we know that he will get off alive, and come to regard them as so many God-sends in the way of book-making.

At worst, travel writing for exoticism and escape would degenerate in the present century to Richard Halliburton as manufactured for the purpose by his publisher—swimming by moonlight in the reflecting pools of the Taj Mahal, for instance. But, as Thoreau suggested, intellectually sophisticated, that is to say, ironic, consideration of the traveler's situation resulted in experience far from naive or vulgar. The reductive ploy of the frontier humorist, the wildly overinflated "sell" practiced upon the incautious egotist, required sharpness and detachment, however sleepily masked. The observing traveler's angle of view, seriously adopted, brought him to detachment and sober astonishment. In both cases the result was what the modern anthropologist has taught us to call the sense of cultural relativism. And that is a sense which befits a realist.

During the four-year sojourn as U.S. Consul in Venice which was the gift of a grateful Lincoln administration, Howells began (not later than 1863) to write the sketches which eventually became his triumphant book *Venetian Life,* 1866. From the beginning the notion of his

sort of travel literature led young Howells to meditate on
the problem of theatrical illusion. Even when you know
it is illusory, even shoddily so, you can succumb to it; but
shoddy convention is not reality. Venice never lost its
charm, Howells testified; but he could not live there three
years "without learning to know it differently from those
writers who have described it in romances, poems, and
hurried books of travel," he said, "nor help seeing from
my point of observation the sham and cheapness with
which Venice is usually brought out, if I may so speak, in
literature." He proposed a Venice not of "dreams—the
Venice of Byron, of Rogers, of Cooper," or "prejudices," or
of "sentimental errors." He proposed to fight his own
temptation to compose "foolish and lying literature." He
proposed a Venice by the light of common day. Often
enough, the resultant reductiveness was playful; but
sometimes the fun became mordant.

Trailing the legend of Paolo Sarpi, for instance, Howells heard the Austrian army holding bayonet practice,
by the numbers, outside the walls of the Servite Convent.
Inside, he saw a rubble of reconstruction smirched by the
night soil of the Venetian poor and dominated by a stack
(perhaps 2,400 cubic feet) of exhumed skulls. But he
could not feel either devout or horrified. Venice was what
it was: "The friars' skulls looked contented enough, and
smiled after the hearty manner of skulls. . . ." And there
was not really much to say except that the whole scene
and system looked foolish. "I could not find that the
ground *was* holy, and it did not make me think of Sarpi,
and I believe that only those travellers who invent in cold
blood their impressions of memorable places ever have
impressions to record," said the traveler, for that moment
a stubborn negative realist.

Subtler, and of course funnier, is the expression of
his ambivalence at first arrival, getting off a frozen Al-

pine express at five o'clock on a winter's morning. In his first gondola,

> The quick boat slid through old troubles of mine, and unlooked-for events gave it the impulse that carried it beyond, and safely around sharp corners of life. . . . But always the pallid, stately palaces; always the dark heaven with its trembling stars above, and the dark water with its trembling stars below; but now innumerable bridges, and an utter lonesomeness, and ceaseless sudden turns and windings. One could not resist a vague feeling of anxiety. . . . Was not this Venice, and is not Venice for ever associated with bravoes and unexpected dagger-thrusts? That valise of mine might represent fabulous wealth to the uncultivated imagination. Who, if I made an outcry, could understand the Facts of the Situation. . . . I felt the liveliest mixture of all these emotions, when, slipping from the cover of a bridge, the gondola suddenly rested at the foot of a stairway before a closely-barred door. The gondoliers rang and rang again, while their passenger
> "Divided the swift mind,"
> in the wonder whether a door so grimly bolted and austerely barred could possibly open into a hotel, with cheerful overcharges for candles and service. But as soon as the door opened, and he beheld the honest swindling countenance of the hotel *portier,* he felt secure against everything but imposture. . . .

Whittier's refugee from cark and care, if he took glamor and the exotic incautiously, had been built up to a treacherous let-down and "sold" into bathos. If he couldn't enjoy the impulse to realism, he wasn't going to like *Venetian Life.* But from the first appearance of Howells's sketches in the *Boston Daily Advertiser* in 1863, they were enjoyed by the nation's most literate and hitherto most seriously romantic audience. The book stayed in print for sixty years. Change had come to travel literature as a genre.

I V

As his chapter on Venice reveals, Twain had not read *Venetian Life* before he wrote *The Innocents Abroad.* He fell into a number of the "sentimental errors" Howells had dispelled. Nevertheless, *The Innocents Abroad* was far from the crude, naive buffoonery critics have often assumed. Howells's perceptive *Atlantic* review in December 1869 insisted that *The Innocents Abroad,* while funny and "charming," proved that "Mr. Clemens" was a writer much better than any transient "popular favorite" or "California humorist" and "entirely different." In the book, Howells said:

> The standard shams of travel which everybody sees through suffer possibly more than they ought, but not so much as they might; and one readily forgives the harsh treatment of them in consideration of the novel piece of justice done on such a traveller as suffers under the pseudonym of Grimes. . . . Yet the man who can be honest enough to let himself see the realities of human life everywhere, or who has only seen Americans as they are abroad, has not travelled in vain and is far from a useless guide.

Seizing on "Grimes" showed acute insight; for "Grimes" as travel writer concentrated in act, style, and attitude every snobbery of race, creed, and culture which could turn a romance-crazed disciple of "Sir Walter Scottism" into a self-righteous monster. Clemens enjoyed the strategic advantages of his *persona* Mark Twain, the inspired idiot. But a defect of the Mark mask was that it obscured the raging compassion, that holy fury against the damned human race, which so deeply and significantly possessed Clemens's imagination. The "Grimes" *persona* as portrayed by the Mark Twain *persona* acted out all the worst Clemens knew about innocents abroad.

Like no few other technical achievements of Clemens's book, his employment of "Grimes" was sophisticated and brilliant. And, as we now know, the ground of that expertise was previous experience. Clemens had exercised the Twain *persona* long and well. In moving from Hannibal to the East, from the printing shops to the river, the river to the mines, and Washoe to San Francisco, he had acquired an immense stock of experience the net result of which became a vision, or at least certain solid glimpses, of the unity of mankind and the meaning of cultural relativism. And that vision had been well developed in the twenty-five travel letters from what were then the Sandwich Islands which he wrote for the Sacramento *Union* in 1866.

In these Hawaiian letters "Mark Twain" was permitted moments of half-serious elevation which enabled him to play a sort of Quixote to the Sancho of a rugged vulgarian styled "Brown." The "Mark" of the *Alta California* letters, which became *The Innocents Abroad,* was a subtler mask surrounded by many foils, only one of which was "Grimes." But "Grimes" helped Howells see that here was indeed a California humorist "entirely different."

With all its innocencies undeniable, Twain's book was still a powerful instrument of negative realism, blending the techniques of frontier humor with those of the disillusioned traveler. After thirty years and more of familiarity, the "Is he dead?" ploy for attacking *ciceroni* seems to me one of the classic instances of American humor, especially as it peaks in Chapter XXVII of *The Innocents Abroad.* The wonderful scenes are too long to quote. But the perfect base-point for them prayerfully breathed forth by "Mark Twain" is brief:

> I never felt so fervently thankful, so soothed, so tranquil, so filled with a blessed peace, as I did yesterday when I learned that Michael Angelo was dead.

Twain is effective in deflating romantic myths like those concerning Petrarch and Laura, Abelard and Heloise, the Parisian *grisettes,* Bedouins, peasants, Americans "cultivated" by travel, royalty, Oriental atmosphere, and Palestinian life styles. His demolition of shameless culture-vulturism applies as perfectly a century later as it did to *Quaker City* "pilgrims" mouthing esthetic hypocrisies before the virtually invisible "Last Supper" of Da Vinci:

> I only envy these people; I envy them their honest admiration, if it be honest—their delight, if they feel delight. . . . But at the same time the thought *will* intrude itself upon me, How can they see what is not visible? . . . What would you think of a man who stared in ecstasy upon a desert of stumps and said: "Oh my soul, my beating heart, what a noble forest is here!"

At once he had struck upon the prime issue of the realists: how are we to *see* things; and by what light? In Venice, Twain could apparently not help seeing what Howells in his way and Hawthorne in his would have taught him: "In the glare of day, there is little poetry about Venice, but under the charitable moon her stained palaces are white again, their battered sculptures are hidden in shadows, and the old city seems crowned once more with the grandeur that was hers five hundred years ago." In the light of common day, Venice looked like "an overflowed Arkansas town," and Twain said he kept imagining "that the river would fall in a few weeks and leave a dirty high-water mark on the houses, and the streets full of mud and rubbish." Presentiments of Bricksville. And which was the reality?

If the humorist and antiromanticist inclined to vote for common day, he could copper his bet, paper over his doubts, by opting for agnosticism. And when doubting Clemens had to take infidel Mark Twain to the Holy

Land, the main goal of the pilgrims of the *Quaker City,* problems of vision and of light to see by became acute. Clemens and the devout—the pilgrims with hearts hardened by security, confidence, and self-righteousness—were riddles to one another. The unco' guid flourished pistols, killed and tortured horses with unscrupulous maltreatment, and resolved at one point to desert a non-devout comrade who fell inconveniently ill. They and Clemens took mutually dim views of one another's morals, but the pilgrims lectured the sinners. In retrospect, a leading saint concluded of Clemens: "He was the worst man I ever knew, and the best." And Clemens, smoking, drinking, swearing, had to come to terms with the idea of the Holy Land under severe conditions.

The result was that Mark Twain faced Palestine, with all its tradition and association, at an angle of vision which saw the holy as very like the romantic. One of the things his imagination found hard to bear was his clear eyes' *reduction* of the land of Biblical and liturgical magnificence. Actuality in the Jordan, the Dead Sea, and the Sea of Galilee shook him:

> Travel and experience mar the grandest pictures and rob us of the most cherished traditions of our boyhood. Well, let them go. I have already seen the Empire of King Solomon diminish to the size of the State of Pennsylvania; I suppose I can bear the reduction of the seas and the river.

From his first glimpse of social realities, Twain recorded his realization that he must "studiously and faithfully unlearn a great many things I have somehow absorbed concerning Palestine. I must begin a system of reduction." He recalled the sonorous magnificence of the phrase "all these Kings" who went out against Joshua to defeat. But the "kingdoms," he saw, must have been mud townships and the "monarchs" petty, ragged sheiks—

"ill-clad and ill-conditioned savages." Presentiments of Tom, Huck, and the gang of robbers.

Nothing could save the Holy Land, he thought, but darkness and romantic glimmer. "Night," he said, "is the time to see Galilee." Its spell turns "feeble in the searching light of the sun":

> In the starlight, Galilee has no boundaries but the broad compass of the heavens, and is a theater meet for great events; meet for the birth of a religion able to save a world; and meet for the stately Figure appointed to stand upon its stage and proclaim its high decrees. But in the sunlight, one says: Is it for the deeds which were done and the words which were spoken in this little acre of rocks and sand eighteen centuries gone, that the bells are ringing to-day in the remote islands of the sea and far and wide over continents that clasp the circumference of the huge globe?

But that was quite as far toward the romance of faith as Mark Twain could go. Shortly he would be brooding over the plain of Esdraelon, where fought the hosts "of Joshua, and Benhadad, and Saul, and Gideon; Tamerlane, Tancred, Coeur de Lion, and Saladin; the warrior Kings of Persia, Egypt's heroes, and Napoleon. . . ." If the "magic of the moonlight" could call from their graves all the phantom armies, what a splendid, ghostly pageant! "But the magic of the moonlight is a vanity and a fraud; and whoso putteth his trust in it shall suffer sorrow and disappointment." Here endeth the lesson.

In the end the important thing appeared to be to avoid becoming Grimes, to eschew the Old Traveler. Though "commonest sagacity warns" that one "ought to tell the customary pleasant lie" about travel, it is important to see, and think, and tell the common truth. Else one is sure of an awful fate:

> The gentle reader will never, never know what a consummate ass he can become until he goes abroad. I speak

now, of course, in the supposition that the gentle reader has not been abroad, and therefore is not already a consummate ass. If the case be otherwise, I beg his pardon and extend to him the cordial hand of fellowship and call him brother. I shall always delight to meet an ass after my own heart when I shall have finished my travels.

Private fantasy Twain authorized: the historical imagination at work, not in public but "in bed, afterward, when . . . in fancy we revisit alone the solemn monuments of the past, and summon the phantom pageants. . . ." Public fantasy he suspected to be asinine posturing. In the light of common day, it must be concluded that "Oriental scenes look best in steel engravings. I cannot be imposed upon any more by that picture of the Queen of Sheba visiting Solomon. I shall say to myself, You look fine, madam, but your feet are not clean, and you smell like a camel."

V

AFTER 1870, THEN, THERE BECAME AVAILABLE TO THE novelist American traditions of realism in fiction as well as continental traditions. The problem would be to transmute the native attack upon people for being what they ought not to be into a presentation and celebration of life honestly seen. The travel vision had to turn and scan life at home, the frontier "sell" be turned inside out. Of the generation of 1870, profoundly gifted in many fields, its novelists Howells, Clemens, and DeForest would develop the native strains over the forty years to come. They would leave a patrimony to generations as distant as those of Faulkner and Auchincloss.

The surprise, once examined, in the tradition is Henry James. Of course, he took modes and models from the continental masters, but he also turned the American sources to canny account. That was part of what Howells meant when, on his own death-bed, he wrote that "James was American to his heart's core to the day of his death. . . . he was never anything but American." Of course it took them all a long time to become serious, positive realists, and James at length moved as utterly through and beyond realism as Clemens. But to fail to grasp James's use, long after and far removed from all beginnings, of the native sources would be to fail in part to read the great work of his middle period.

The figure for James's development toward *The Portrait of a Lady* is curiously spiral. Perhaps there was a warring ambivalence between the romanticism of his heart's compulsion to Europe, to the life of "impressions," and the devotion of his mind and eye to serious vision, serious art. Though the great eye flashes through it once in a while, *Transatlantic Sketches* is on the whole an embarrassment. Its defensive *persona* of a passionate pilgrim runs panting after the picturesque with less critical detachment than even Fenimore Cooper or Washington Irving. Yet Howells was right: James's true eye shared the American vision.

The American stands as an endlessly fascinating case in point. How can it be so bad when it is so good: and vice versa? Ultimately it seems not likely that any critic can answer that double-edged question so well as James himself in his preface to the volume as revised for the New York edition. *The American* is so good because the young author's fine, careless rapture in creativity opened for him a "season of images so free and confident and ready that they brush questions aside and disport themselves, like the artless schoolboys in Gray's beautiful Ode, in all the ecstasy of the ignorance attending them." But it is bad because the rapturous author innocently failed to see that his "conception unfurled, with the best conscience in the world, the emblazoned flag of romance. . . . arch-romance. . . ." Unwittingly, in the best of faith, he lied to himself and his reader because he meant and said "reality" while he composed "romance."

Not, of course, that the mature James thought romance a bad thing on its own ground; and in explaining the situation in the 1910 preface to *The American* he said some of the best and deepest things ever recorded about the distinction. "The real represents . . . the things we cannot possibly not know. . . . The romantic stands, on the other hand, for all the things that, with all the facilities in the world . . . we never *can* directly know." Again, romance deals with "experience disengaged, . . . exempt from the conditions that we usually know to attach to it . . . and operating in a medium which relieves it, in a particular interest, of the inconvenience of the *related,* a measurable state, a state subject to all our vulgar communities." And so James proceeded to his justly famous trope of real experience as a captive balloon and the romancer as the artist who "for the fun of it" cuts the cable and sends us soaring into "the disconnected and uncontrolled."

James saw that he had cut the cable by falsifying the family Bellegarde. He confessed to the recognition that really it was all romance. But he undertook, wrongly, to save *The American* for himself and the Edition by ultimate reliance on the "more or less convincing image" of Christopher Newman. As one suspects James himself of seeing, Newman, considered as a "steeping the whole matter in the element of reality" on James's own terms, won't do either. The fascinating thing is the Americanness of imagining Newman as an innocent abroad, the impulse to try to do what in *The American* James could not yet bring off. Though it was intrinsically the artist's *donnée* in *The American* that Christopher Newman should be a self-made Western tycoon, James's ignorance of the qualities of such a man doomed his creator to foregone failure. To contrast James's Westerner with Owen Wister's makes one gasp at the irony. What a pity Wister had really no notion what to *do* with his Virginian. And how intriguing James's compulsion to include the established figure of the American innocent in his own primal esthetic equation.

But when James imagined an innocent abroad whose psychology, manners, temperament, motives, and morality he understood, she would be Isabel Archer, the stuff of greatness. As he proposed in his notebook, for all her independence and even as the penalty of her finest qualities of courage and idealism, "The idea of the whole thing is that the poor girl, who has dreamed of freedom and nobleness, who has done, as she believes, a generous, natural, clear-sighted thing, finds herself in reality ground in the very mill of the conventional." From that point forward the native sources of American realism would be transmuted into the created characters of genius, characters exactly like those recipients of James's letters of whom, in the perspective of more than fifty years, Howells noted that they were "more largely American than most Americans might think, though American of European texture and color, but alike in the civilization which we share surprisingly with the English and incomparably with the French." An American thus joined the ranks of the continental masters, and the native sources ran at last in the mainstream of Western culture.

5 / Huckleberry Finn

by Common Day

IN THE LIGHT OF COMMON DAY, WHICH WAS CHARACTERIS-
tically Clemens's light, his masterpiece appears more
realistic than a reading of the bulk of critical discussion
during the past two decades would give one warrant to
believe. *Adventures of Huckleberry Finn* by common
light looks different (older and perhaps fresher) and
more securely a masterpiece than some schools of judgment allow. Perhaps one cannot say that the great book
is realism or only realism. But it may be worthwhile to
see how it looks in certain contexts of its school and moment.

Not to repeat what has been well said by Henry Nash
Smith and Harold Kolb, *Huckleberry Finn* is a brilliant
hybridization of the major sources of native realism—of
"frontier humor" in the full flowering of its vernacular
tradition, its war against pretentiousness, its skill in the
reductive techniques of the "sell"; and of the American
travel book in its maturely antiromantic phase, with its
insights into the meaning and importance of cultural
relativity. It is, however, upon the triumph of Twain's
novel in wedding an ancient, even archetypal, genre to a
brand new, contemporaneous genre that I wish to focus.

In a number of central, fateful ways the novel is a picaresque (meaning, for purposes of this discussion, a work of fiction in the tradition of the literature of roguery). It is also a *boy-book* (a book written not so much for the entertainment of boys as for the purpose of exploring and defining the experience—and its significance—of the American boy).

I

WHILE IT HAS LONG BEEN A COMMONPLACE TO OBserve that *Huckleberry Finn* is picaresque, criticism has tended to let that go at mere notice and hurry to more fashionable concerns. If the great novel has roots in Clemens's marvellous biography, it is also true that we really do not possess a psychology adequate to explication of creative processes, or even to describing the imagination. And a major danger attendant on the biographical fallacy in criticism is that the readable work will be sacrificed to a forlorn hope thrown against the inscrutabilities of creative inwardness. We have the work, all of it we are going to get. The work has its integrity which we must respect; and the defensible aim of enquiry and judgment can at last only be to learn to read it better. Further, the essence of literary greatness is not "originality" *ex nihilo* but the power to filter and assimilate imaginative nutriment out of the intellectual biosphere and convert it into some distinct and significant newness. Clemens achieved that essence with his use of the picaresque tradition in *Huckleberry Finn,* and one reads it better by realizing how.

Actually, its roots in the picaresque appear to be among the novel's tap-roots to human universality. As a genre the picaresque took its name from the modes of *Lazarillo de Tormes* and *Guzman de Alfarache* with their swift-following developments in English and French literature. Ambiguously heroic, Lazarillo, Jacke Wilton, Guzman, and Gil Blas are generically "rogues"—tricksters, diddlers, vagabonds, scoundrels, confidence men, and victims of poverty, social scorn, hard knocks, and shifty morals. The literary picaro has been, from Lazarillo forward, a deceptively simple-seeming but sophisticated esthetic resource. He can be handled narratively from an apparently neutral or disapproving point of view which permits the author to employ him for radically critical purposes. The picaro is a bum, a man underground who looks up at the seamy undersides of the world. Through his eyes a subversive author can show us the follies and vices of mankind—or of particular men representing an Establishment—yet offer a face of conformity or innocence to the censor; after all, are these not the views of a detestable rogue? Slyly, too, the artist can be sure of audience response to one of the reliable delights of mankind—vicarious escape from pressure and restraint, from fear of all the ills that flesh is heir to, especially civilization and its discontents.

From babyhood we revolt against restraint, repression, authority, and standards of action, thought, or sensibility. Even when by internalizing standards we have become civilized, we continue to be divided against ourselves, revolt beating at the bars of inhibition. Therefore our delight in the great picaros from Falstaff to W. C. Fields rises from delight in the success of a projected, a safely illusionary triumph over repression. Vicariously we step outside the moral strictures of our lives, flout and violate them with impunity. In actuality we could not bear either to suffer from or be a rogue with outrageous freedoms; and that is what makes for our delight.

Taking the foregoing as true opens the way to consider that of course they did not invent the picaro in

Spain or, indeed, in literature. He is preliterate, that is to say folkloristic; and he is prehistorical, that is to say mythological. Greek legends like those of Zeus against Kronos or Odysseus the godlike confidence man are paralleled not only by the Norse Loki but any number of the myth-heroes of primitive cultures who portray the Promethean picaro, a culture-hero daring, resourceful, defiant of ancient scruple, who has stolen or tricked away from the inscrutable, awful Lords of Life the essentials of human existence: fire, corn, sunlight, breadfruit or whatever is indispensable. No matter what else these virtually universal myths mean, it seems clear that they take their rise as devices of the human imagination for coping with the too much, for expressing man's sense of survival by the skin of his teeth against the vast menace and mystery of the Powers. Through mythic picaros man gets even, imaginatively, with the universe.

Culturally speaking, long before literature could matter to Clemens the classical tradition of myth heroes had been buried in such reductive mockery as Irving's account of the Battle of Fort Christina. But the picaresque was neither dead nor inane. It lived vigorously with the folk. One of the pervasive motifs of folk-story is that of "Puss in Boots," or "The Minstrels of Bremen," or Twain's great favorite "Brer Rabbit." There the weak, the disarmed, dispossessed, exposed, and exploited win out miraculously over the powerful and terrible by luck, flair, and wit. Peasant cultures, slave or serf cultures, produced folk-heroes standing for the suppressed and despised against the dominant, the "approved," the officially "civilized." Or, of course, the situation might be reversed and an Establishment writer, perhaps a threatened conservative, produce satiric "picaros" (Socrates in *The Birds*, Jack Cade or Bottom the weaver in Shakespeare) to illustrate the necessity and justice of old ways.

Altogether, it may be said that there exist three general sorts of picaros in the broad tradition: sympathetic picaros originally out of myth and folklore; antipathetic picaros out of aristocratic satire; ambiguous picaros out of the literature of covert subversion. Every variety of picaresque may be said, in present-day terms, to be a fiction of the Absurd.

The literary and aristocratic picaresques proved congenial to American writing from the start and have continued in force from Trumbull's *Progress of Dulness* and Brackenridge's *Modern Chivalry* through Don Marquis's *archy and mehitabel* and Bellow's *Adventures of Augie March*. But the American tradition was far from limited to the literary. The frontiersmen of the Atlantic beachhead imported with them European tensions between folk and official culture, and almost at once they added the deep conflicts inherent in black slavery. On the frontier these foregone generators of the picaresque were reinforced by a new confrontation with nature and a new, inescapable conflict of cultural dignities. In Europeans and their children brought suddenly up against the wilderness an awareness of natural menace was revived which had slept in legend for centuries. Bears, catamounts, alligators, rattlesnakes—and who knew what other monsters?—became real tests of the psyche. Even in pastoral Westchester, when the men were gone during the Revolution wolves came and gnawed the frozen apples on the dooryard orchard ground. Nature bred, mysteriously, violence and terrible stress in the conflicts of continental and subtropical climates. Heat, cold, disease, starvation, savage warfare—the struggle with nature and the unknown became real again and led to the development of imperfectly recorded figures who were more or less folk-heroes and almost culture-heroes.

Larger, stronger, more courageous than life, they laughed (in the imagination) at menace and coped easily with nature and all the pains of "uncivilization": Boone, Brer Rabbit, Mike Fink, Crockett, Johnny Appleseed, Pecos Bill, John Henry.

Coping with "civilization," however, laid another, often infuriating, set of stresses on frontier folk. From its Atlantic beginnings the frontier as a cultural condition was placed in a position of at first desperate, then galling dependency on Europe and "home." Dependency built up in colonials the cultural inferiority complex reactions of subserviency on the one hand and defensive rebelliousness on the other. And as the edges of civilization—achieved agriculture—moved West, frontier emotions moved with them, adding to the established irritations at Europe a twin difference with the towns across the mountains, the East. The factual referents of frontier emotions were many and complex. Economic and political exploitation were real, but so was dependency on capital and public investment. Frontier losses of traditional culture were real, though frontier creativity meant something. Frontier leveling, opportunism, and personal freedom grated on civilized nerves; "civilized" disapprobation, decorum, profit-taking, and tourism struck the frontier as snobbish, hypocritical, and heartless. Imagination on the frontier undertook to get even by such devices as the critical wit of the tall tale and "sell," the just-folks ploys of the Pike, Puke, Hoosier, hick and hillbilly, and by an extraordinary American recreation of the picaresque.

When Howells concluded that Clemens was "the Lincoln of our literature," one of his implications was that both ultimate Americans had been reared in "Western" culture. As Lincoln supremely incarnated the life-style of plain people, Clemens elevated it to high art. Both knew and reveled in the mind which created such picaros as Sam Slick, Simon Suggs, and Sut Lovingood and opened the way to fame for Artemus Ward, Josh Billings, and Bill Nye. Twain became the master of the American revels, the great artist who could realize at once upon the charm of the American picaresque and upon its potential for crushing critical impact. Since for him there was nothing at all of a genteel tradition in the picaresque, he was to the manner born, he could assimilate for imaginative purposes the European tradition as easily as the native mode and knew, at least preconsciously, how to connect them both to questions and answers forever recurrent in the condition of man.

If, therefore, every main sort of picaro appears in *Huckleberry Finn*, there is still to consider a great literary tradition, closely allied to the picaresque and in American practice assimilated to it: quixotism. Without edging too far into the literary wars of the Spanish succession, it is probably safe to say that there are certain obvious likenesses between the Spanish picaresque and *Don Quixote*. Both operate to reduce and deflate romantic superhumanism, to level it down to the realms of poor human flesh and blood. In Cervantes as in all his followers mad knights are counter-pointed against earthy squires for critical purposes; and the everlasting Sanchos have a tang about them of the rogue. Twain was of much the same mind as Trumbull in *M'Fingal* and Brackenridge in *Modern Chivalry* when he praised *Don Quixote* as the first book that "swept the world's admiration for the mediaeval chivalry-silliness out of existence"; and even more than *Moby-Dick* Twain's novel abounds in knights and squires.

Effective variations on picarism and quixotism run

through every portion of *Huckleberry Finn.* Starting in the first four chapters with the nonsense about Tom Sawyer and his gang, Twain plays Knights and Squires over and over. Huck plays Sancho, the deflating Squire to Tom's inflated Knight. Later Jim plays Squire to Huck's Knight; then Huck to Buck Grangerford; then Huck and Jim to the Duke and the Dauphin; and at the last, in a complex triangle, Tom, Huck, and Jim play Knights and Squires intermingled with a travesty upon *The Count of Monte Cristo.* Cervantes' formula was, of course, time-tested and foolproof. It is commonplace—right and necessary—to observe that characters play Don Quixote and Sancho in Twain's novel. What is less commonplace, but informative, is to notice that in playing knights and squires they play roles presenting the negative and positive realisms well established among the literary modes of the day.

Southerner as he largely was, Clemens blamed the ills of the South upon romanticism, specifically that of Sir Walter Scott. The American and French Revolutions, he said, had left the world in debt for "great and permanent services to liberty, humanity, and progress. Then comes Sir Walter Scott with his enchantments, and by his single might checks this wave of progress, and even turns it back; sets the world in love with dreams and phantoms; with decayed and swinish forms of religion; with decayed and degraded systems of government; with the sillinesses and emptinesses, sham grandeurs, sham gauds, and sham chivalries of a brainless and worthless long-vanished society. He did measureless harm; more real and lasting harm, perhaps, than any other individual that ever wrote. . . . Sir Walter had so large a hand in making Southern character, as it existed before the war, that he is in great measure responsible for the war."

I I

IF PICARISM AND QUIXOTISM BELONGED TO ANTIQUE modes refreshed by frontier experience, the other genre which informed *Huckleberry Finn* was an immediate creation of Clemens's generation. The American boy-book, a distinct literary type, sprang unpredictably from the brow of Thomas Bailey Aldrich. *The Story of a Bad Boy* was topped by *The Adventures of Tom Sawyer*, transmuted in Howells's *A Boy's Town*, but brought to swift greatness in *Adventures of Huckleberry Finn*. In Stephen Crane's *Whilomville Stories*, W. A. White's *Court of Boyville*, and Tarkington's *Penrod* series (to mention only high points) the genre became permanently established. There can be few parallels in history for the virtually simultaneous creation of a significant and very popular genre by a trio of close friends; but enquiry into the reasons why is more important for the light it throws upon the books than for the satisfaction of historical curiosity.

The motivating impulses behind the creation of a new fiction to study and express the nature of boyhood seem to have been blended of a sense of cultural discontinuity and a prescientific psychologism bred from realistic tendencies. Aldrich makes an intriguing case because, as the years went on and the esthetic-intellectual wars waxed hot, he opted for the genteel tradition, the camp of the "idealizers." But in 1869 he began the primal boy-book, saying, "I call my story the story of a bad boy, partly to distinguish myself from those faultless young gentlemen who generally figure in narratives of this kind, and partly because I was *not* a cherub. . . . I didn't want to be an angel and with the angels stand. . . . In short, I was a real human boy . . . and no more like the impossible boy in a story-book than a sound orange is like one that has been sucked dry." The obvious motive is that of negative realism; the implied motive, to present a boy as the creatures are, looked to positive realism and the obliteration of Bronson Alcott's theory of the child.

In Clemens's most important comment on the genre, written to Howells right after *Tom Sawyer* was finished, he made it clear that he distinguished between the boy-book and what we call the growing-up novel and that he thought of the boy-book in relation to the picaresque. He intentionally didn't, says Clemens of Tom, "take the chap beyond boyhood":

> I believe it would be fatal to do it in any shape but autobio-graphically—like Gil Blas. I perhaps made a mistake in not writing it in the first person. If I went on, now, if I took him into manhood, he would just be like all the one-horse men in literature & the reader would conceive a hearty con-tempt for him. It is *not* a boy's book at all. It will be read only by adults. It is only written for adults.

And later in the same letter, looking forward from 1875 to *Huckleberry Finn,* he remarks, "By & by I shall take a boy of twelve & run him on through life (in the first person). . . ." If Clemens's audience prognostication was faulty, his idea was clear. Boyhood is different, a human condition distinct from, perhaps better than, manhood, something decidedly worth an artist's attention.

But how could the artist get at boyhood? Obviously only through memory, the power Howells thought most essential to a novelist, his accumulated store of sight and insight. Clemens was, typically, more explicit, even abso-lute. "A foreigner," he wrote, "can photograph the exteri-ors of a nation" but no more:

> I think that no foreigner can report its interior—its soul, its life, its speech, its thought. I think that a knowledge of these things is acquirable in only one way, not two or four or six —*absorption;* years and years of unconscious absorption;

years and years of intercourse with the life concerned; of living it, indeed; sharing personally in its shames and prides, its joys and griefs, its loves and hates, its prosperities and reverses, its shows and shabbinesses, its deep patriotisms, its whirl-winds of political passion, its adorations— of flag, and heroic dead, and the glory of the national name. Observation? Of what real value is it? One learns peoples through the heart, not the eyes or the intellect.

There is only one expert who is qualified to examine the souls and the life of a people and make a valuable report —the native novelist. This expert is so rare that the most populous country can never have fifteen conspicuously and confessedly competent ones in stock at one time. This native specialist is not qualified to begin work until he has been absorbing during twenty-five years. How much of his competency is derived from conscious "observation"? The amount is so slight that it counts for next to nothing in the equipment. Almost the whole capital of the novelist is the slow accumulation of *unconscious* observation—absorption. The native expert's intentional observation of manners, speech, character, and ways of life can have value, for the native knows what they mean without having to cipher out the meaning. But I should be astonished to see a foreigner get at the right meanings, catch the elusive shades of these subtle things. . . . Does the native novelist try to generalize the nation? No, he lays plainly before you the ways and speech and life of a few people grouped in a certain place—his own place—and that is one book. In time he and his brethren will report to you the life and the people of the whole nation. . . . And when a thousand able novels have been written, *there* you have the soul of the people, the life of the people, the speech of the people; and not anywhere else can these be had. And the shadings of character, manners, feelings, ambitions, will be infinite.

Such notions of the creative source had in turn their sources, I think, in a feeling which is perhaps ambiguously realistic: the acute nostalgia which the constant acceleration of everything Henry Adams meant by "multiplicity" brought to minds which had in boyhood known village simplicities. One cannot understand the contemporaneous popularity of "Snow-Bound" or its appeal even now to previously uninitiated readers without recognizing Whittier's avowed aim:

> Clasp, Angel of the backward look
>> And folded wings of ashen gray
>> And voice of echoes far away,
> The brazen covers of the book;
> The weird palimpsest old and vast,
> Wherein thou hid'st the spectral past. . . .
> Even while I look I can but heed
>> The restless sands' incessant fall,
> Importunate hours that hours succeed,
> Each clamorous with its own sharp need. . . .
>
> Yet, haply, in some lull of life,
> Some Truce of God which breaks its strife,
> The worldling's eyes shall gather dew,
>> Dreaming in throngful city ways
> Of winter joys his boyhood knew . . .
>> These Flemish pictures of old days;
> Sit with me by the homestead hearth,
> And stretch the hands of memory forth
>> To warm them at the wood-fire's blaze!

Howells in 1874, only months before he began the prodding of Clemens which eventuated in "Old Times on the Mississippi," had printed in the *Atlantic* "While the Oriole Sings," a fine account of a flash of memory back to childhood occasioned by hearing an oriole sing from John Fiske's garden. Childhood scenes, games, fears, irrelevancies flow by, and the poet's reflections are at once realistic and nostalgic:

> Ah, nothing, nothing! Commonest things:
>> A touch, a glimpse, a sound, a breath—
> It is a song the oriole sings—
>> And all the rest belongs to death.

But oriole, my oriole,
  Were some bright seraph sent from bliss
With songs of heaven to win my soul
  From simple memories such as this,

What could he tell to tempt my ear
  From you? What high thing could there be,
So tenderly and sweetly dear
  As my lost boyhood is to me?

The men of the age had an uncomfortable feeling, which is easier to understand in 1970 than it seems to have been in 1920, that just around the corner of their own lives they and their age had let slip something precious.

With such notions in the atmosphere it is not entirely a mystery that the realists took up the boy-book or that Clemens found his high creative vein in "the Matter of Hannibal." There was an operational sense in which realism, picarism, quixotism, and the feeling of cultural discontinuity could blend and become mutually supportive in the boy-book. *Adventures of Huckleberry Finn* demonstrated that fact. Out of the intellectual climate of the time, moreover, there came to the boy-book writers two conceptions which did not materially change between Aldrich and Tarkington. One is a blend of conjectural history with Darwinism: that, psychogenetically, ontogeny recapitulates phylogeny, and from child to boy to man the youth passes through evolutionary stages of savagery and barbarism into civilization; that boys are natural savages. The other is a cognate, pre-Freudian psychology which conceives neither of psychodynamics nor of the search for identity. The psychology of the boy-book appears to conceive of personality, even character, as given and static, determined possibly in babyhood but mainly by inheritance and alterable, if at all, in passage from the plateau of one condition of man to another. The boy is not there imagined to "mature" in any sense paral-

100

lel to our psychological notions, and he *has* his identity. At best he learns to see, he becomes more or less enlightened. At worst he only surrenders boyhood to become another contemptible "one-horse" man. His personality does not change dynamically in response to experience, and it is useless to demand that it do so.

One of the most interesting aspects of the boy's condition will be his natural war with civilization. A savage, detached and mutinous, a boy is a kind of sympathetic picaro, an ardent member of an underground conspiracy to elude the tyrannies of official, respectable society. His disengaged eye may be formidable; but he is properly a savage with the immunities of his condition and promise, at worst and best "a bad boy."

I I I

THE FORM OF *ADVENTURES OF HUCKLEBERRY FINN* IS analogous to the shape of what is called a "block-I" The work consists of a long central narration, picaresque in form and substance and framed on either end by boy-book narratives. There is not a plot in the book so much as a series of actions ("box-car" or "beads-on-a-string" construction), and the actions serve varying purposes—presentational, critical, or technical—in the novel as a whole. The "author" is, as the second sentence tells us, "Mr. Mark Twain." But "Mr. Twain" does not appear in the book except as the writer of the introductory "Notice"; and Samuel L. Clemens, the creator of Mark Twain, does not appear except perhaps as the author of the second prefatory note, "Explanatory," on the dialects. Since, as Clemens had planned for a decade, the narrative point of view is "autobiographical," with Huck Finn telling us everything in the language of dramatic report, summary, or revery, I find it hard to determine the answer to questions about "the implied author."

For pluralistic as well as esthetic reasons, as we have seen, realists were concerned first and last with character, sacrificing every fictional consideration to present their vision of personhood. Technically the choice of a first-person narrator presents the artist from the beginning with a crux. Shall the teller be primarily an "I-narrator" or an "eye-narrator"? Shall the stress fall primarily on what the narrator sees, on what his vision reveals to us? Or shall it fall on how the observer-narrator responds and changes in response to outward events? On the whole, I should suppose the method of Joyce's *Ulysses* to be mainly illustrative of the self-conscious "I-narrator." Twain, prompted by realism, by his age's concept of the static psyche, and by the traditions of the picaresque, chose to present Huck largely as a lens to furnish us a sharper vision of otherwise unknowable reality. To use Jamesean terms, Huck "registers" for us, and "reveals." Because he can take us "inside" his own mind and emotions, he can expose himself as a figure of emergent moral reality, though not a maturing or altered personality. What we see through his eyes are a fresh, immediate, wonder-laden boy's world of nature and boy-life side by side with a rogue-riddled world of social failure and decadence.

The first three chapters, connecting with the boy-life of *Tom Sawyer,* begin subtly to introduce two themes: negative realism and the problem of "civilization." The original cover and title page of the book gave its full title as *Adventures of Huckleberry Finn (Tom Sawyer's Comrade);* and from the beginning Tom's "comrade" plays Sancho to Tom's Quixote without fail. The boys are, naturally and forgivably, God's romantic fools and God's picaros. A little older, they might become what Twain recalled of himself at twenty—chuckle-headed, "a callow fool, a self-sufficient ass." A little older yet, "one-horse" men. But what would be despicable in men is sympathetic in boys. They can be robbers, Robin Hoods, vicarious heroes of toweringly bloody, absurd romance: and they are so, even Huck, except that Huck is often too ignorant, a "sap-head," to know how to enjoy the immunities of romance and forever brings a lethally pragmatic intelligence to bear. No quixotism can help Huck see camels and elephants, a caravan laden with diamonds, in a primer class's Sunday School picnic. Without malice, with a Sancho's phlegm, he concludes "that all that stuff was only just one of Tom Sawyer's lies. I reckoned he believed in the A-rabs and the elephants, but as for me I think different. It had all the marks of a Sunday-school."

Tom's romanticism formed the easier half of the "civilization" which oppressed Huck, however. Life with the Widow Douglas and Miss Watson turned out so "dismal regular and decent" he ran away, and only Tom could get him to go back. Eventually, though, Huck began to like housekeeping ways and began to learn in school that "six times seven is thirty-five." But he was apprehensive. Pap was sure to come back. And with chapter four begins the first of five main actions contained within the boy-life frame of the novel. Throughout them things happen to a largely passive Huck. For the most part he does not plan and does not move until he has to. But things happen. And in the first episode, which spans chapters four through seven and might be called "Pap against Civilization," it is the return of Pap which snatches the novel away from mere boy-life and negative realism.

Early in the novel, especially, no admiration can be too extravagant in appreciation of its fictional "business" scenes, Twain's transitions. They are glorious: Huck turning to Miss Watson's Jim for a little conjuring and their solemn foisting off of Huck's counterfeit quarter on Jim's magic hairball; Huck's escape from Pap's cabin; Huck succeeding after all in conning essential intelligence from canny Judith Loftus. The studies, the ingenuities, the wealth of power lavished on vision, characterization, drama, speech, language, just to move the action along—one can say only that such technique is the overflow of a gusher of genius.

Certain incautious speculations about the novel have supposed that Twain intended it to become a general indictment of civilization in favor either of primitivism or the frontier. They seem to have ignored Pap. If life at the Widow's had been itchy and dismal, even to his son Pap was horrible:

> His hair was long and tangled and greasy, and hung down, and you could see his eyes shining through like he was behind vines. . . . There warn't no color in his face, where his face showed; it was white; not like another man's white, but a white to make a body sick, a white to make a body's flesh crawl—a tree-toad white, a fish-belly white. As for his clothes—just rags, that was all.

Pap was a real rogue close to the end of his road. He was a thief and a drunk, illiterate, filthy, full of howling hate against blacks, schools, cleanliness, and respectability, a con artist, and a sadist who cowhided and licked Huck with his "hick'ry" until he "was all over welts" and feared for his life. Pap was a man with nothing to show for the frontier experience but the experience of cultural erosion.

On the one hand, back with his Pap Huck could find things "lazy and jolly" and "pretty good times up there in the woods"; on the other, he scarcely got away with his life. If the counter and opposite to "civilization" were taken to be Pap, there would be much to say for town, school, and the Widow. Easy boy-life evading the cramps of civilization was one thing; real life with a real picaro was something else. Huck opted out and skipped out on both, "murdering" himself and running and hiding to drop even below the town bum's level, clean out of sight and legal being. He became technically a nonperson for the duration of the long, central section of the novel.

Escaping to use Jackson's Island as a hideout, Huck could play lonesome, autonomous Robinson Crusoe, monarch of all he surveys, until he stumbled upon his man Friday—Miss Watson's Jim, who had become another legal nonperson, a fugitive slave. And here of course begins the second main action of the novel ("Jim against Civilization"), and we are presented with a third major tension to interact with and complicate all the rest. It will not do, the novel will not warrant it, to suppose Jim a "Black Christ." The novel's actual point would have seemed far more significant to Clemens, anyway: Jim is a man, altogether human, a person entitled to the dignities and compassions pertaining to personhood. But even Jim, as Woolman and Jefferson had argued must inevitably be true of a slave, was a bit of a picaro. His mighty brag about his witch's ride and his hairball swindle suggest that he is, like the boys, a sympathetic rogue but no saint. He is a man of warmth, authenticity, and dignity which are amazing not for their superhuman dimensions but their power to survive slavery and for the force with which they confound the stupid contempt of a smug slave civilization.

What unites the comrade of Tom Sawyer in solidarity with the despised and technically criminal black man is their lost, defiant, underground condition, their unpersonhood in the eyes of established society and its standards. His at-one-ness with Jim remains to the end a source of trouble and guilt to Huck. How can the comrade of Tom Sawyer be living and chumming with a black man? The comrade's answer is, because he is really unworthy of Tom, being so ignorant, lowdown, and ornery as he is, dragged up as the son of the town drunk and bum, a boy that never had no show. The conditions of Huck and Jim become polar to society and its civilized standards. The unspoken problem, the potential morality not moralized, the issue developing toward eventual revelation is the ever more strained and ironic tension between those poles: one condition or the other must be wrong, must at last be condemned as not only absurd but evil.

When Huck, moving "as hard as I could go," bursts into the cave exclaiming, "Git up and hump yourself, Jim! There ain't a minute to lose. They're after us!" his personal identification with Jim has been unpremeditatedly solidified to a degree which no subsequent event or meditation could dissolve. And the next group of chapters, perhaps just barely unified enough to be an episode ("Huck and Jim"), seems to me to have been taken out of context by some criticism. Going down the river on a raft in chapters twelve through sixteen restores to Huck familiar pleasures of Crusoeness and boy-picarism. Huck does say, "we lived pretty high"; but he had liked it in the sugar hogshead and Pap's cabin. The actual proportion between pages devoted to feelings of security and natural idyll and pages devoted to other things in this section of the novel is two to thirty-nine. The other things are terror, wreck, lostness, natural menace, failure, and disaster. It wasn't likely that an author of Clemens's generation would take seriously the notion of idyllic nature, and he did not. After Darwin there were few reasons to suppose that nature might be a safe and pleasant haven or that, like Emerson's poet, one could retire to his own green hills alone where man in the bush with God might meet. It seemed more likely that one might meet competition, suffering, and extinction in the bush; and nothing in Clemens's experiences of nature on the river or in the West had given rise to romantic expectations. Like the pilot's cub in "Old Times on the Mississippi," Huck had to learn to read the river; and what he read was hard, disillusioning stuff.

The most significant dramas in this third section of the book are two which portray moments when Huck succumbs to boyishness and the lure of Tom Sawyerism, when he tries to play the Don to Jim's Sancho. Seeing by lightning flashes the carcass of a steamboat wrecked on a rock and likely to wash away at any moment, Huck fires up with the idea of boarding and looting her. He persuades reluctant, sensible Jim by asking, "Do you reckon Tom Sawyer would ever go by this thing? Not for pie, he wouldn't. He'd call it an adventure—that's what he'd call it. . . . And wouldn't he throw style into it?—wouldn't he spread himself, nor nothing?" But when it turns out to be a real, not a boy's adventure; when they discover real cutthroats, not boy picaros on board the *Sir Walter Scott*, the adventure turns out to be an experience of sickening terror, no fun at all. Reality on the river is no joke.

Something of the same thing is true of the next adventure, which the author paced beautifully into Huck's narrative. Inevitably, part of the loot from the *Sir Walter Scott* consists of romanticistic fiction which Huck reads aloud to Jim about "kings and dukes and earls and such, and how gaudy they dressed, and how much style they put on." Jim is fascinated but, playing Sancho, not much impressed with royalty. He sees mighty sensible reasons for being less than convinced by the majesty or wisdom of Solomon and proves to Huck that he can outdo him at logic. We are prepared for the eventual entry of the Duke and the Dauphin; but, more immediately, we are pre-

pared for the scene in which Huck's intellectual acceptance of Jim becomes final. Separated in a fog, they fight
all night to find each other in a terror of blind lostness.
When Huck finally does find the raft he catches Jim
asleep, exhausted by labor, vigil, and grief. A devil of
Tom Sawyerism and perhaps some pique at losing his
argument possesses Huck. He ignores Jim's joy at reun-
ion, persuades him that the danger was all a dream,
tempts him into a wild interpretation of the dream, then
lets him see that it was a joke, a "sell," and that Jim has
been tricked, made a fool of.

Jim's reaction is a revelation to Huck. Jim's emotions
are real, and Jim offended has dignity. Jim is a real person. Huck's evidence that Jim has been fooled is a litter
of "leaves and rubbish on the raft and smashed oar" from
the wild night of crashing into invisible tow-heads. Huck
trips Jim's too eager interpretation with them, and Jim
answers "steady without ever smiling":

> "When I got all wore out wid work, en wid de callin' for
> you, en went to sleep, my heart wuz mos' broke bekase you
> wuz los', en I didn' k'yer no mo' what become er me an de
> raf'. En when I wake up en fine you back agin', all safe en
> soun', de tears come en I could a got down on my knees en
> kiss yo' foot I's so thankful. En all you wuz thinkin 'bout
> wuz how you could make a fool uv ole Jim wid a lie. Dat
> truck dah is *trash;* en trash is what people is dat puts dirt
> on de head er dey fren's en makes 'em ashamed."

> Then he got up slow, and walked to the wigwam, and
> went in there, without saying anything but that. But that
> was enough. It made me feel so mean I could almost kissed
> *his* foot to get him to take it back.

> It was fifteen minutes before I could work myself up to
> go and humble myself to a nigger—but I done it, and I
> warn't ever sorry for it afterwards, neither. I didn't do him
> no more mean tricks, and I wouldn't done that one if I'd 'a'
> knowed it would make him feel that way.

After that, though scraps of "conscience" from a slave-holding "civilization" scorch him, Huck employs his finest picaresque talents to lie and connive and save Jim from slave-catchers until the river gets them. A steamboat runs smashing over the raft, and Huck comes up from a deep dive to avoid the paddle-wheel and finds Jim and the raft apparently gone forever. He swims ashore to stumble into the most poignant and perhaps significant of his adventures, with the Grangerford-Shepherdson feud, constituting the fourth major action of the novel.

As we look down the great valley with Huck in a year sometime near 1840, the finest representatives we meet of what purports to be its civilization are the Grangerfords. They are gentry; and there is much to be said for them. They are clean, slim, handsome, courageous, generous, disciplined and by their lights honorable and cultivated Christian ladies and gentlemen. The tragedy is that in certain essential respects their light is darkness. After the knightly code of honor had degenerated into the *code duello* among European gentry, the code was sure to degenerate a step lower to the noncodes of shooting on sight and bushwhacking on the frontier. And so the feud possessed these best of citizens like a disease. In them civilization had murderously turned into anticivilization. The same could be said for the fate of the ideals of Castiglione: the arts of the courtier had become the gorgeous absurdities of a genteel romanticism. Huck's innocent accounts of the art of Miss Emmeline, especially the obituary of Stephen Dowling Botts, provide the finest and funniest castigations of sentimentality and Byronic strut ever achieved by a negative realist. But by the end of the episode, in two wonderfully *realized* chapters, the Grangerford-Shepherdson feud has become a Missouri *Romeo and Juliet* illustrating not merely aristocratic pride and greed for eminence but the agonies of an obsolete, vicious Sir Walter Scottism. Decayed romanticism has turned the best people in the book, in the region, suicidally irrational. Huck covers up his slain comrade's face and cries "a little" and moves on. There is nothing else to do.

Back on the raft, which hidden-out Jim has of course refurbished, life seems lovely for "two or three days"—especially since Huck and Jim do not sweat about the fact that, Cairo and the free states long gone by, Jim is going nowhere. And then the major picaros arrive, one jump ahead of the dogs and a lynch mob, and Huck naturally takes them aboard the raft. Here, at chapter nineteen, begins the final major action of the central core of *Adventures of Huckleberry Finn.* What could be called "The Duke and the Dauphin" contains four subepisodes to illustrate their preposterous roguery.

"It didn't take me long," says Huck, "to make up my mind that these liars warn't no kings nor dukes, at all, but just low-down humbugs and frauds. But I never said nothing, never let on": he knew where he was. "If I never learnt nothing else out of Pap, I learnt that the best way to get along with his kind of people is to let them have their own way." As events turn out, Huck's shrewd judgment has the defects of a boy's lack of forecast. Letting the rapscallions have their way will put Huck's life in danger and get Jim sold back into bondage; but technically it lets the central action of the novel surge forward.

As the last spinal episode of *Adventures of Huckleberry Finn,* "The Duke and the Dauphin" constitutes a brilliant picaresque. Here it becomes clear that the loose, shaggy progressions of the ancient form and the ironies traditional to its equivocal tone and point of view perfectly match the author's needs. Introducing the rogues on the raft and recounting their sack of Pokeville, Clemens "plays it" upon us his readers with dismaying skill. Our vicarious release through identification with the scoundrel in action is joyful. But at Bricksville we are brought up sharply, sickeningly, by a glimpse through the veils of fun and safety into tragic evil.

It is, I think, essential to see that, in some small defiance of chapter divisions, the adventure of "Bricksville" is all one action from the introduction in chapter twenty-one of the rapscallions' wonderful Shakespearian travesty to the summing up by Huck toward the end of chapter twenty-three: "Sometimes I wish we could hear of a country that's out of kings," and (of the Duke and Dauphin) "you couldn't tell them from the real kind." The elements of the adventure are: the shooting of Boggs and its aftermath; the circus; and "The Royal Nonesuch."

Problems of tone and perspective throughout "Bricksville" are extraordinarily complex—and rich. In spite of a great deal of modern-day longing to the contrary, Huckleberry Finn never is John Woolman. As a boy and as our perspective upon the action, Huck is an innocent but no bleeding heart. He has not quite learned to read the river. His compassion for old man Boggs's daughter is exceeded by his concern for the "drunk" circus rider, and his enthusiasm for the king "cutting shines" almost matches his delight in the circus. It is never clear that Huck makes much more of a distinction among the three "circuses" than the village loafers. Morally, that is all right for a boy, especially Huck, the picaresque son of a picaro, an innocent, sympathetic picaro, son and associate of antipathetic, guilty scoundrels. His condition makes him an ideal, and in "Bricksville" a virtually transparent, lens. But all the opposites are true for the rogues and their marks, the men of Bricksville. Their condition is evident at a glance. They are totally devoid of the satisfactions of civilization. The loafers perish about the slimy street, scrounging chaw-tobacco, dying for excitement, any relief from their horror of ennui: a dog-fight, torturing a dog to death, a fight, a shooting, a lynching—anything! And the Duke and the Dauphin are just the boys to give it to them, for a price. The picaros know how to "work" Bricksville. They know all the moves in advance because they know what is the matter. Without civilized reality, Bricksville is sick of rotten romanticism.

The circus is fine for a boy—innocent fantasy for the innocent. But the circus provides a foil and a curiously complex objective correlative for the Bricksville tragedy, the shooting of Boggs, because it reveals that Bricksville has no sense of human reality. One circus is as good as another; at last the real shooting and abortive lynching become only modes of entertainment: there is no reality. Sherburn shoots Boggs and Boggs insists upon getting shot because both are victims of Sir Walter Scottism—a disease, obviously, of the region's middle classes as well as its aristocracy. And when the mob comes to lynch him, Colonel Sherburn tells them what they really are: cowards, dupes, and silly dreamers. "Now the thing for *you* to do is to droop your tails and go home and crawl in a hole," Sherburn advises the men of Bricksville; and they do it.

The smashing success of the rapscallions' "campaign" with three nights of "The Royal Nonesuch" and their clean getaway with the loot tells us why Sherburn is right and what the situation means. Unable to score with fake Shakespeare, the king and duke promise salacity. The biggest line on their poster says, "LADIES AND CHILDREN NOT ADMITTED"; and, as the duke remarks, " 'if that line don't fetch them, I don't know Arkansaw!' " But he does know, and foresees exactly their reactions to his "sell." How does he know? Because he understands the ancient rules of picarism, which are much like the ancient rules of the gypsy and other confidence men. There's a little larceny in every human heart and so, although you can't cheat an honest man, you can gull almost anybody somehow. And what those con men know about their society is that, perishing of boredom, sodden in Sir Walter Scottism, it will do almost anything for a sufficiently attractive fantasy, no matter how absurd or destructive.

After "Bricksville" we come back to human reality with Jim, an authentic adult, a man, grieving over real losses. Though Huck says he understands Jim, the words he speaks suggest that the degree of his empathy has sometimes been overestimated:

> I know what it was about. He was thinking about his wife and his children, away up yonder, and he was low and homesick; because he hadn't ever been away from home before in his life; and I do believe he cared just as much for his people as white folks does for their'n. It don't seem natural, but I reckon it's so.

Then Huck reports the heartbreaking story of Jim's discovery that his "little 'Lizabeth" was deaf and dumb. I cannot feel that one ought to suppose that Huck's distancing of himself from Jim here is consciously or strategically ironic on Huck's part. There is biting human irony here, but it is the novel's irony, the author's irony, of which Huck serves as an instrument and in part the boy-innocent butt.

The irony is in fact only visible (as in the work of a realist it should be) to the reader and his perspectives. The irony is that the false, empty, stupid and grotesquely illusioned caricature of a "civilization" represented by Bricksville should presume to hold in chattel bondage and contempt a real man like Jim. In Huck's next adventure that irony is multiplied by the silly vulnerability to the duke and king of the Wilks family and most of the citizens of their nameless village. What "fetches" them so thoroughly that the picaros almost pull off a major confidence game, which includes swindling orphans and selling slaves off down the river, is a travesty of romantic sentimentality. Huck's language, because this is one disease of adult and feminine emotional life to which a boy is immune, tells us everything: "sobbing and swabbing," "tears and flapdoodle," "rot and slush," "all that soul-butter and hogwash." The upshot is that, though the deadbeats go too far and see their game bust, the self-condemnation of the "civilization" is made complete when the Wilks women, honest, generous women, reveal their moral idiocy. Clemens may not, even during this final caper of the Duke and the Dauphin, have yet decided upon the damnation of the human race. But there remains no doubt as to his novel's conclusion about the proslavery South.

That conclusion, it seems to me, is the nail driven home by Huck's famous meditation after the picaros, desperate for whiskey, have "played it" on him too:

> I thought till I wore my head sore, but I couldn't see no way out of the trouble. After all this long journey, and after all we'd done for them scoundrels, here was it all come to nothing, everything all busted up and ruined, because they could have the heart to serve Jim such a trick as that, and make him a slave again all his life, and amongst strangers, too, for forty dirty dollars.

The stages of Huck's thought are worth tracing. He thinks that Jim would be better off home, "as long as he'd *got* to be a slave," and he'd better write home. But he gives up the notion because (a) Miss Watson would "sell him straight down the river again" and, even if she didn't, "everybody naturally despises an ungrateful nig-

ger" and Jim would always "feel ornery and disgraced";
and (b) everybody would find out that "Huck Finn helped
a nigger to get his freedom" and he'd be justly shamed.
All at once, and in the precise language of the fundamentalist conversion-experience which dominated the regional religion, Huck enters a crisis of conscience. Not
yet meaning to become "good," he makes a discovery:
"You can't pray a lie." So, "full of trouble" and con-
founded, he decides in fact to repent, to turn Jim in. At
once his burden rolls away, and he feels "light as a
feather. . . . good and all washed clean of sin for the first
time I had ever felt so in my life."

But then Huck reflects in terms neither social nor
religious, only human, about Jim the person, the self-
sacrificial friend, the man he protected from slave-catchers, and crisis returns. He picks up the letter to Miss
Watson which had made his act of contrition and instrument of salvation, and he considers:

> It was a close place. I took it up, and held it in my hand.
> I was a trembling, because I'd got to decide, forever, betwixt
> two things, and I knowed it. I studied a minute, sort of
> holding my breath, and then says to myself:
> "All right, then, I'll *go* to hell"—and tore it up.
> It was awful thoughts and awful words, but they was
> said. And I let them stay said; and never thought no more
> about reforming. I shoved the whole thing out of my head;
> and said I would take up wickedness again, which was in
> my line, being brung up to it, and the other warn't. And for
> a starter, I would go to work and steal Jim out of slavery
> again; and if I could think up anything worse, I would do
> that, too; because as long as I was in, and in for good, I might
> as well go the whole hog.

Couched in the language of evangelical "testimony,"
Huck's was the problem, as old as Abraham and Anti-
gone, of conflict between a "good" conscience and a
"right" conscience. The novel's irony reaches its peak, as

115

everybody knows, when Huck (an innocent with every reason to believe that he really has chosen sin, death, and eternal torment) chooses rightly, morally, humanely in defiance of the legally, officially, theologically sanctioned "civilization" around him. The book is calculated, through irony, to make us feel that in fact what Huck rejects is neither civil nor humane but perverse, absurd, and uncivilized, a vicious nonsense which every sound heart, clear mind, and conscience undeformed ought to spurn. The point should be lost on no reader that Huck achieves this moment of superficially confused but actually, and ironically, accurate moral vision because he is a boy not reconciled to civilization and a picaro's boy "brung up" to "wickedness."

The irony resolves, of course, exactly opposite to Huck's supposition. This is his climax, but he is saved by it, not damned. "Civilization" is damned; in the context of the whole novel it is totally damned. The only saving, enduring ground of civilization is that pitying, loving human heart which takes poor human nature, as King Lear and the best work of Hawthorne and Melville had taken it, as Howells and Stephen Crane took it, to be ultimate in itself.

I V

ALTHOUGH AS A CHARACTER HUCK APPEARS IN A SIZable number of other works, *Adventures of Huckleberry Finn* is weighty and significant beyond comparison with any of the others. Its greatness stems not from the charm or importance of Huck as a character (though he has become the object of a rather complicated and romantic personality cult). Its greatness stems from the intellectual dimensions of the book, and these are rooted in the critical irony which deepens from chapter five through chapter thirty-one, where Huck recants and chooses hell. Since the intellectual, the critical, the moral, perhaps the metaphysical (if such exist in this book) movements of the novel peak in chapter thirty-one, why did the author not stop there? Why did he go on through the final eleven chapters of Tom Sawyerish farce and bathos? Firmly rejecting even such apologists as Lionel Trilling and T. S. Eliot, the majority verdict of contemporary criticism has been that the final section of the novel is an esthetic disaster, or almost so.

Is there anything else to be said? From the present point of view, yes; there is something to say which explains why to at least one reader the ending of *Adventures of Huckleberry Finn* has never seemed ruinous and why it never seemed difficult to agree with Eliot: "it is right that the mood of the end of the book should bring us back to that of the beginning. Or if this was not the right ending for the book, what ending would have been right?" It makes a great deal of difference what one takes the book to be, what expectations one is prepared to insist that the book fulfill.

Huckleberry Finn is a triumph of its genre and not some other. It is not an epic nor a tragedy. It is not *Paradise Lost* or *King Lear* or *Moby-Dick,* though it shares certain of their insights into the human condition. Because it is a great work of the literary imagination, it speaks to us and our condition; but it speaks neither from the romantic ground which the sensibility of our times prefers nor from the Alexandrian ground of "well-made" art preferred by our much-structured criticism.

When the author's imagination was done with its critical dissection of the Sir Walter Scottish, chuckleheaded and criminal Old Southwest, his principal remaining problem was to know what to do with Jim. As has often been observed, the revealing journey down the

117

river had been a voyage to nowhere, in practical terms an absurdity, for Jim. To kill him off or even leave him a fugitive in darkest America would have turned the book toward *Uncle Tom's Cabin,* toward romance and sentimentality. In the formal traditions of picarism, however, it did not necessarily matter whether the novel ended or where. The picaresque tones of farce and absurdity made anything possible. And the boy-book did not formally climax. It couldn't because, sweet as boyhood might be, losing it had to be supposed natural, inevitable, and right—no tragedy, just a fade-out from boy-life to a succeeding stage. Finally, the view and sensibility of the realist led to the conclusion that good art only cuts into a moving stream of life and need not misrepresent it by climax or resolution.

Therefore, I suppose, *Adventures of Huckleberry Finn* legitimately returns upon itself to end as it began in boy-life. Not changed, not even much sobered (he has, after all, resolved upon a permanent life of crime), Huck is delighted to see Tom Sawyer and have his help in "stealing" Jim from the Phelps Farm. Since there can no longer be much point to taking "civilization" seriously, the author, narrator, and reader can laugh and play along with Tom Sawyerism while the book modulates away from tragic implications and returns to its proper tone.

The proper tone was bathos and the proper technique anticlimax. How else could Jim be imagined, as of 1840, to be got safely home, as the proprieties of a comic fiction require? Perhaps Clemens let himself be run away with by Tom Sawyer and there is too much farce—it becomes a somewhat narrow issue of taste at last. With all the farce and parody, all the antiromantic japes, has the integrity of Huck's developed soul been broken? I cannot think so. He is what he was and, never imagined to grow up, must always be: "Yours truly, Huck Finn." Has Jim's authentic dignity been violated, a more serious charge? I do not think so because no man could have his dignity genuinely threatened by a comic phantasmagoria and because his last real action stands as one of the few bits of unmistakable heroism in the book, when he returns himself to bondage, possibly death, to help the doctor care for wounded, delirious Tom Sawyer.

At the end of the ends, I would read by the lights of boy-book and picaresque even Huck's too-famous final remark: "I reckon I got to light out for the Territory ahead of the rest, because Aunt Sally she's going to adopt me and sivilize me and I can't stand it. I been there before." It is a boy-remark in a boy-book context, not a commitment to destiny. At its most significant, perhaps it pointed the way to those further "adventures" on which the author would indeed send Huck. But his new adventures were to be minor just as an Aunt Sally sort of civilization is trivial. The critical work, the major ironic work, of *Adventures of Huckleberry Finn* once done neither could nor needed to be done again The book remains to us to read, each by his own best light.

6 / "The Wizard Hand":

Hawthorne, 1864-1900

"**H**AWTHORNE APPALLS, ENTICES . . ." SAID EMILY DICKIN-son in 1879, rather surprisingly striking the note of response standard among the first generation of serious American readers after Hawthorne's death. They saw in their great romancer something uncanny, perhaps morbid, perhaps sublime, certainly exotic, piercing, and supremely artistic. In Hawthorne his native land had somehow produced an authentic genius. The obituary poetry all said "sorcery." Over Hawthorne's grave Longfellow lamented,

> The wizard hand lies cold. . . .
> The unfinished window in Aladdin's tower
> Unfinished must remain!

Bronson Alcott echoed,

> Painter of sin in its deep scarlet dyes,
> Thy doomsday pencil Justice doth expose,
> Hearing and judging at the dread assize;
> New England's guilt blazoning before all eyes,
> No other chronicler than thee she chose.
> Magician deathless!

And the much less orphic Dr. Holmes recalled, from the Saturday Club, "The Essex wizard's shadowed self. . . ."

> The great ROMANCER, hid beneath his veil
> Like the stern preacher of his sombre tale;
> Virile in strength, yet bashful as a girl,
> Prouder than Hester, sensitive as Pearl.

Finally, E. C. Stedman, aiming at a definitive public verdict, summed up in 1877:

> Two youths were fostered in the Norseland air,
> One found an eagle's plume, and one the word
> Wherewith a seer divines:
> Now but the Minstrel lingers of that pair,—
> The rod has fallen from the Mage's hand.

I

IN THE SELF-CONSCIOUS UNITED STATES, BREATH-takingly expanding after the war, Hawthorne was bound to achieve the status of a national treasure. His works passed through edition after edition. Articles by the dozen of Hawthorne reminiscence and association clustered into a personality cult. At more serious levels the great romancer became the first true native challenge to American criticism. How ought he to be elucidated? Not only an inspiration, he was a mine of suggestion for American aspirants to his art. And his work came to serve as a critical touchstone for the judgment of successors. Hawthorne's became the first unquestionably major American fictional reputation.

The tale of Hawthorne's editions between his death in 1864 and the close of the century is told in Volume IV of Jacob Blanck's monumental *Bibliography of American Literature*. James T. Fields, the publishing paragon of an age of steam, pushed Hawthorne hard. "Little Pansie" appeared in three forms, and *Twice-Told Tales* in a "Blue and Gold" edition during 1864–65, followed by Sophia Hawthorne's notoriously edited version of the *American Note-Books,* 1871, in a market sequence carefully spaced. Then it was time for James R. Osgood, having succeeded Fields, to continue with family editions of *Septimius Felton,* 1872, *The Dolliver Romance* and then *Fanshawe and Other Pieces* in 1876, and, scraping the barrel clean at last, *Dr. Grimshawe's Secret,* 1883.

Canny management of manuscript, and of magazine in relation to book publication, thus kept Hawthorne in some sense a current author for two decades after the last publication of his personal lifetime. At length the moment arrived for the ultimate monument, the definitive set, edited by George Parsons Lathrop, Hawthorne's son-in-law, and published by Houghton Mifflin, successors in turn to Osgood: *Writings of Nathaniel Hawthorne,* in twelve volumes, 1883.

If all this left no doubt of Hawthorne's prestige, the rest of his publishing history in the period makes clear his popularity—and market value. Osgood made the point with sixteen Hawthorne issues in "Little Classic" editions, and Houghton Mifflin drove it home with "Modern Classics" and "American Classics for Schools." Hawthorne had become "a classic" and was to be published without cessation. Into the 1880's, as the "Textual Introduction" to the Centenary Edition makes clear, *The Scarlet Letter* was reprinted "with an impression or more almost every year."

About such a figure, given the traditions of nineteenth-century genius-worship and the exigencies of American cultural nationalism, there quickly clustered a literary personality cult. The wizard mysteries of Hawthorne's life, personality, and art lent themselves to exploitation. Some of this was mere gossip, some ordinary self-advertising of the Hawthorne-Knew-Me sort. Much of it consisted of association and locale mongering, though it provided some serious and relevant biographical material. But the genuine reminiscence was concentrated in a run of major articles and, finally, books which within fifteen years after his death certified Hawthorne's genius.

The themes for discussion of Hawthorne during this period were largely set by E.P. Whipple's "Nathaniel Hawthorne," first published in 1860 but reprinted in *Character and Characteristic Men,* 1866. It was surrounded by a growing set of significant pieces, especially George W. Curtis's "The Works of Nathaniel Hawthorne" (*North American Review,* October, 1864), Elizabeth Peabody's "The Genius of Nathaniel Hawthorne" (*Atlantic,* September, 1868), Eugene Benson's "Poe and Hawthorne" (*Galaxy,* December, 1868), Dorville Libby's "The Supernatural in Hawthorne" (*Overland,* February, 1869), the *Southern Review*'s "Writings of Nathaniel Hawthorne" (April, 1870), solid book chapters in James T. Fields' *Yesterdays With Authors,* and the English *Memoir of Nathaniel Hawthorne* (by "H.N. Page," [Alexander Japp]), both 1872. Perhaps the final cachet became that imprinted beside Hawthorne's name by a famous English author generously writing for an American magazine: Anthony Trollope, "The Genius of Nathaniel Hawthorne" (*North American Review,* September, 1879).

In the perspective of these and dozens of estimates of Hawthorne slighter or more oblique, however, it seems clear that only with the publication of three major works between 1876 and 1879 did Hawthorne become an unchallengeable American genius. The first of these was a pioneering systematic examination and evaluation determinedly entitled *A Study of Hawthorne* by George Parsons Lathrop in 1876. The second and most famous was the almost reluctant concession of a brilliant but alienated critic: Henry James's *Hawthorne*, 1879. The one now least known but possibly then most significant was E.C. Stedman's public ode, "Hawthorne," 1877.

Invited by the Phi Beta Kappa society of Harvard to deliver a thirty-minute poem, Stedman had devoutly contemplated "The College of the Gods" but felicitously settled upon "Hawthorne" for his subject. As his authorized biography puts it, Stedman essayed to be "our most popular American Poet of Occasion, the Universal Official Poet, as it were, upon whom a large neighborhood reliance was placed for an illuminating, artistic, sympathetic, even prophetic, expression of the dominant spirit of the ideal." The role was one in which Whitman and Lanier failed lamentably. And by invading Harvard for the purpose Stedman put himself into competition with the local experts—Lowell and Holmes—in the practice of a now little-understood Old American art form: democratic Pindarics, meant bardically to essentialize the highest truths of the national consciousness and so to crystallize them for the guidance and uplift of the nation —in this case of the national taste.

Hawthorne he placed boldly beside Longfellow as equally a poet, though really the more prophetic of the two: "The one New-Englander!—New England's best interpreter, her very own." Nurtured amid wilding beauty but disciplined in solitude, "Two natures in him strove/ Like day with night, his sunshine and his gloom." For exercise of "His mysterious gift" the world could well afford that "one" should "meditate aloof" and ignore "the time's heroic quarrel." For "none save he in our time so laid/ His summons on man's spirit . . ."

What if he brooded long
On Time and Fate,—the ominous progression
　Of years that with Man's retribution frown,—
The destinies which round his footsteps throng,—
Justice, that heeds not Mercy's intercession,—
　Crime, on its own head calling vengeance down,—
Deaf Chance and blind, that, like the mountain-slide
　Puts out Youth's heart of fire and all is dark!
What though the blemish which, in aught of earth,
　The maker's hand defied,
Was plain to him,—the one evasive mark
　Wherewith Death stamps us for his own at birth!

Ah, none the less we know
He felt the imperceptible fine thrill
　With which the waves of being palpitate,
Whether in ecstasy of joy or woe,
And saw the strong divinity of Will
　Bringing to halt the stolid tramp of Fate;
Nor from his work was ever absent quite
　The presence which, o'ercast it as we may,
Things far beyond our reason can suggest:
　There was a drifting light
In Donatello's cell,—a fitful ray
　Of sunshine came to hapless Clifford's breast.

Flatulent as Stedman's verse now seems, his diary
entry at concluding its composition is pathetic: "I *think*
the poem is at my highwater mark—as sustained, analytic, and imaginative, a piece, as I shall ever write." It
was analytic. It alluded continuously to Hawthorne's
work. It took positions on most of the contemporaneous
issues of the Hawthorne criticism—standing with Fields
and Lathrop against Curtis's attack on Hawthorne's politics; with Whipple, Peabody, and Lathrop on the prophetic power of Hawthorne's imagination, the bardic
quality, even, of his prose; with Japp and Lathrop against
Whipple on the balance of Hawthorne's mind and character; with Lathrop on the historicity and profundity of

Hawthorne's treatment of Puritanism, his evocation of the spiritual essence of New England. Always, in fact, Stedman stood with Lathrop. "Hawthorne" poeticized Lathrop's *Study,* accepting it as definitive. An epigone of the dying age of romantic idealism, Stedman felt authorized to set Hawthorne up on the plinth of his poesy by the romantic notion that beauty and genius, ideality and art, heroism, misty rhetoric and windy euphony all went together.

"Hawthorne" foreshadowed the end of an age which faded into agonizingly extended tenuities. With every allowance for taffy, it is astonishing to hear Dr. Holmes praise its "admirable contribution . . . to our poetical and our critical literature," or Aldrich class it with Arnold's "Thyrsis," or Julian Hawthorne call it "the most true and beautiful tribute yet made to Nathaniel Hawthorne's genius" by one of the two "best poets now living." Ideality, whether as decayed romanticism or desperate neoromanticism, was to be long a-dying. And the reputation of Nathaniel Hawthorne during the balance of the nineteenth century was to be continuously involved in the struggles to keep ideality breathing.

I I

DETAILED EXAMINATION OF EARLY HAWTHORNE CRITicism would show it engaged from work to work in a good deal of expostulation and reply over minor issues. But the theme of permanent significance is the still vexed problem of the nature of reality in Hawthorne's work and mind. No question was more central to either the literary or the philosophic battles over ideality. And none was so central to the point of view or achievement of Henry James's *Hawthorne.* Speculation on the question had of course begun during the romancer's lifetime. It had become acute after Whipple, only apparently to be resolved by Lathrop. James shattered Lathrop's resolution. In doing so he projected Hawthorne criticism decisively toward the Realism War of the '80's and '90's.

Whipple, whose work Richard Fogle has called perhaps "the purest example extant of the Victorian development of Romantic organicism," was a pioneering exponent of what we now perceive as a Melvillean insight —that Hawthorne's distinctive vision revealed "the power of blackness." A decayed Christianity, thought Whipple, Puritanic Law with no compensating Grace, provided the key to Hawthorne's "peculiar mind," which "touches the lowest depths of tragic woe and passion—so deep, indeed, that . . . Jonathan Edwards, turned romancer . . . could not have written a more terrific story of guilt and retribution than *The Scarlet Letter*."

Not so, replied Elizabeth Peabody and Alexander Japp: Hawthorne's was a valid, if ecclesiastically liberated, Christianity. Lathrop carried the rebuttal to a peak of appreciation—effectively blending his own intuition of Hawthorne's mind with his own sense of Hawthorne's art. Hawthorne, he said, "had not the realistic tendency, as we usually understand that, but . . . the power to create a new species of fiction." And "the kind of romance that he has left us differs from all compositions previously so called." It is not the "romance" of Scudéry or Fielding, or the German Romantics. "It is not the romance of sentiment: nor that of incident, adventure, and character viewed under a worldly coloring: it has not the mystic and melodramatic bent belonging to Tieck and Fouqué."

There are, Lathrop holds, two things which "radically isolate" Hawthorne's art. These are, first, "its quality of revived belief":

> Hawthorne . . . is a great believer . . . his belief goes out
> toward what is most beautiful, and this he finds only in

moral truth . . . This unsparingly conscientious pursuit of the highest truth, this metaphysical instinct, found in conjunction with a varied and tender appreciation of all forms of human or other life, is what makes him so decidedly the representative of a wholly new order of novelists.

But is Hawthorne not usually thought to be a sceptic unbeliever? That arises, Lathrop answers, only from a superficial "appearance of doubt" and "his fondness for illuminating fine but only half-perceptible traces of truth with the touch of superstition . . . And out of this questioning belief and transmutation of superstition into truth . . . proceeds also that quality of value and rarity and awe-enriched significance, with which he irradiates real life until it is sublimed to a delicate cloud-image of the eternal verities."

Lathrop's Hawthorne thus becomes a genius of vital ideality—a "fictionist" who "penetrates . . . far into individual consciences" and provides "a profoundly religious aid" for many readers. Thence Lathrop prepared to issue a transcendent claim for his American genius:

> Hawthorne's repose is the acme of motion; and though turning on an axis of conservatism, the radicalism of his mind is irresistible; he is one of the most powerful because most unsuspected revolutionists of the world. Therefore, not only is he an incalculable factor in private character, but in addition his unnoticed leverage for the thought of the age is prodigious. These great abilities, subsisting with a temper so modest and unaffected, and never unhumanized by the abstract enthusiasm for art, place him on a plane between Shakespeare and Goethe.

About the decision whether to undertake his *Hawthorne* for Macmillan's English Man of Letters series, Henry James may or may not actually have said "again and again," as Julian Hawthorne claimed in his *Memories:* "I don't want to do it. I'm not competent: and yet, if

I don't, some Englishman will do it worse.... Your father was the greatest imaginative writer we had, and yet, I feel that his principle was wrong; there is no more powerfully and beautifully written book than *The Scarlet Letter*, and yet I believe the whole conception of it was wrong! Imagination is out of place; only the strictest realism can be right." But there can be no doubt that Hawthorne, and still more Lathrop's Hawthorne, presented the James of the late 1870's with painful as well as intellectually formidable challenges.

James's only sustained, book-length, and independent literary study, his *Hawthorne* takes on a peculiar significance in the context of its moment of Hawthorne criticism. If the first two chapters shed a dim light on Hawthorne, they provide a justly famous documentation of the then current state of mind of Henry James. In one aspect, as a work of criticism James's book is shockingly bad: it is so mincingly self-conscious, so provincially deprecatory in its determination to maintain a "European" point of view and in its implied dismay at Lathrop's intolerable Yankee brag—Hawthorne on a plane between Shakespeare and Goethe, indeed! But in another aspect James's is a great, free, original critical achievement.

Both the strength and the weakness of his *Hawthorne* sprang from James's alienations. However necessary to his creative success, even survival, his sorely won expatriation, the need to justify himself to himself made James a blind, supercilious biographical and cultural critic in *Hawthorne*. But his intellectual alienation from his father's idealism, in brief his own agnosticism and his commitment to the wholly this-worldly vision of the secularized continental realism then bitterly controversial and "modern," endowed James's view of Hawthorne's mind and art with piercing originality. With mocking ambiguity, James refuses to perceive the existence of Lathrop's unique romancer. Not believing in Puritanism, says James, Hawthorne simply did not believe. Not believing, he treated the matter of Puritanism "from the poetic and aesthetic point of view, the point of view of entertainment and irony." Metaphysically, Hawthorne was "a man of Fancy . . . with a kind of small ingenuity, a taste for conceits and analogies," a mind easily prey to "allegory . . . one of the lighter exercises of the imagination," and a bore.

"It cannot be too often repeated," James insists, "that Hawthorne was not a realist." His people "are all figures rather than characters." Hawthorne persistently deserted (James almost says "betrayed") his natively high sense of the real, of actuality. As he soars into moonlit tenuity, "we get too much out of reality, and cease to feel beneath our feet the firm ground of an appeal to our own vision of the world—our observation." The result is that in the long run Hawthorne becomes to James "a beautiful, natural, original genius" of an almost pure but rather irresponsible artistry. His art is "original and exquisite" and unique: "No one had had just that vision of life, and no one had had a literary form that more successfully expressed his vision."

Yet in the end, James the realist could not take seriously the ideal white magic of the wizard hand. The exasperation of a rebel modernist and secularist shines through the deprecation, even the patronizing, of James's conclusion:

> He was not a moralist, and he was not simply a poet. The moralists are weightier, denser, richer. . . . He combined in a singular degree the spontaneity of the imagination with a haunting care for moral problems. Man's conscience was his theme, but he saw it in the light of a creative fancy which added, out of its own substance, an interest, and, I may almost say, an importance.

Even from the sympathetic Howells, James's book brought the observation that for the Bostonian reaction to some of James's remarks he waited "with the patience and security of a spectator at an *auto da fé,* to see." Howells protested that fairness to Hawthorne demanded a recognition, deliberately withheld by James, of the traditional difference in esthetic intention between the romance and the novel. To idealists and romanticists, however, attitudes like James's were infuriating. But there was no real point of leverage for their wrath until, quite innocently, Howells provided it in a famous essay, "Henry James, Jr.," of 1882 which initiated the American phase of the Realism War and plunged Howells, James, and Hawthorne into the semantic middle of a bitter logomachy.

Howells's essay raised such a storm of obloquy and, as effect led on to effect, delivered him into a warfare so sturdy that it is easy to forget how mild and obvious were his opinions: "It seems to me that an enlightened criticism will recognize in Mr. James's fiction a metaphysical genius working to aesthetic results. . . . The art of fiction has, in fact, become a finer art in our day than it was with Dickens and Thackeray. . . . The new school derives from Hawthorne and George Eliot . . . ; but it studies human nature much more in its wonted aspects, and finds its ethical and dramatic examples in the operation of lighter but not really less vital motives." It responds to "the realism of Daudet rather than . . . Zola"; and "this school, which is so largely of the future as well as the present, finds its chief exemplar in Mr. James," to whom "we cannot deny . . . a very great literary genius."

Howells in the same piece wondered if James himself were not most truly a romancer: "his best types have an ideal development," but "perhaps the romance is an outworn form, and would not lend itself to the reproduction of even the ideality of modern life." To the ultimate chagrin of James, however, one of the unfairnesses of the succeeding controversy became the fastening of the label "realist" or "modern realist" firmly to "Howells-and-James," as notoriety coupled them. Then there ensued the sort of confusion of terms inevitable to intellectual warfare. It was recalled that in philosophic tradition Realist (the opposite of Nominalist) meant Idealist. It was pointed out that the "modern realist" was an agnostic if not a materialist. And it was said with scorn and venom that these "moderns" were prophets of a false, antispiritual, anti-ideal, perhaps vicious "reality."

Inevitably, the Hawthorne of Lathrop was taken to represent the cause of the True Realists; Hawthorne the sceptic, Hawthorne the disengaged artist, the Hawthorne of James, became the model of the modernists. Inevitably, criticism of Hawthorne as well as the regular passing reference to Hawthorne, of the sort which constitutes the substance of genuine fame, became loaded with this distinction—and with its confusions. And, since the Lathropian Hawthorne was by far the more puissant figure and because such a figure was essential to the idealists, the idealist Hawthorne figured much more frequently. Certainly neither the Hawthorne criticism of the '80's and '90's in either England or the United States nor the general literature of criticism and controversy over fiction in the period can be read accurately without attention to these problems of tactics and terminology.

In general the idealists and agnostics, however customarily unfair as to personalities, were correct in their understanding of the intellectual and esthetic issues: the realist-agnostics were in revolt against the ideal; the romancer-idealists did look toward the substance of things hoped for and not of the seeable world. The neoromantics, who wanted romantic (or, as Howells distinguished them, "romanticistic") sensations divorced from romantic faith, constituted a third and mischievous force. "I hold with the poets and the idealists, not the idealizers, but those who have ideals," said Charles Eliot Norton in 1895. Although George Pellew had argued that "An honest return . . . to the point of view of the early romanticists is now impossible," nevertheless "Scott and Hawthorne and Thackeray," William Roscoe Thayer insisted, tell us from on high: "The Real includes the Ideal, but the Real without the Ideal is as the body without life, a thing for anatomists to dissect." One champion of neoromanticism, H.C. Vedder, was so far carried away as to suggest that George Washington Cable might be superior to Hawthorne, for the latter is "psychological rather than moral, an observer and analyzer of moral problems, and coldly critical, not sympathetic. . . ." But it was to be in that very probing intellect that the realists found Hawthorne's strength. Said Howells in *My Literary Passions* (1895):

> . . . none of Hawthorne's fables are without a profound and distant reach into the recesses of nature and of being. He came back from his researches with no solution of the question . . . but the awful warning, 'Be true, be true,' which is the burden of *The Scarlet Letter*. . . . It is not his fault that this is not intelligence, that it knots the brow in sorer doubt rather than shapes the lips to utterance of the things that can never be said.

I I I

BY THE 1890'S THESE MAJOR (AS WELL AS A NUMBER OF minor) themes were firmly set as background for the treatment of Hawthorne in periodical criticism, book or part-book length studies, occasional poems, even the early texts and school histories of American literature. Particularly with regard to developments in the international and historical novels and the literature of local color, Hawthorne's example served steadily as an authorization and incitement to writers and inevitably as a critical touchstone. Sampling of reviews, to say nothing of critical commentary in every form, suggests that hundreds of testings of the literature of the age by the Hawthornian touchstone might be found. Indeed, it suggests that a minor critic might well have doubted his respectability if he failed to cite Hawthorne whether in praise of or attack against any writing in question. Howells, concluding that Hawthorne had left "a legacy which in its kind is the finest the race has received from any mind," felt moved to continue wryly, "As I have said, we are always finding new Hawthornes, but the illusion soon wears away, and then we perceive that they were not Hawthornes at all; that he had some peculiar difference from them, which, by-and-by, we shall no doubt consent must be his difference from all men ever more."

A large but profitable study in itself would be that of the influence of Hawthorne on the American fiction writers of this extended generation. Everyone agreed that Hawthorne was a master stylist—an American master of English, or perhaps even a master of American English. Mark Twain, listing in 1879 the national treasures which entitled Americans to be indifferent to British national contempt, climaxed his list with the comment: "Nobody writes a finer and purer English than Motley, Howells, Hawthorne and Holmes." And, in a characteristic "whoop of joy" at the discovery of an esthetic experience, William James wrote to Henry on January 19, 1870, of his delight in reading *The House of the Seven Gables:*

> I little expected so great a work. It's like a great symphony,
> with no touch alterable without injury to the harmony. It
> made a deep impression on me and I thank Heaven that
> Hawthorne was an American. It also tickled my national

feeling not a little to notice the resemblance of Hawthorne's style to yours and Howells's. . . . That you and Howells with all the models in English literature to follow, should needs involuntarily have imitated (as it were) this American, seems to point to the existence of some real American mental quality.

Though Mark Twain found Hawthorne nevertheless one of the people whom it just tired him to death to read, authors so various as Bellamy and Cable, Jewett and Tourgée, James Lane Allen and the followers of F. Marion Crawford devoted themselves to revival of the Hawthornian romance. And, as we have seen, Hawthorne's impact upon the realists was profound. Though a fragmentary literature on the subject exists, no one has yet truly elucidated the ways in whch James and Howells, as features of their very rebellion against "the Mage," repeatedly created—and in psychological, moral, and even mystical as well as esthetic developments—significant variations upon themes by Hawthorne.

After the triumph of a foolish neoromanticism over tho realists in their battle for American public taste during the '90's, the serious idealists and the realists drew closer. Howells pointed out "the difference between the romanticistic and the romance, which is almost as great as that between the romantic and the realistic. Romance, as in Hawthorne, seeks the effect of reality in visionary conditions; romanticism, as in Dickens, tries for a visionary effect in actual conditions." And with the work of the great realistic internationals all turning toward the psychological, even the psychic, the Americans, in the same currents, found it easier to be reconciled to Hawthorne—though Henry James's latest comment as a formal critic on Hawthorne was only less dry than the conclusion of his early book. In an article for the *Library of the World's Best Literature,* 1897, James recalled only that Hawthorne was "an aesthetic solitary. His beautiful, light imagination is the wing that on the autumn evening just brushes the dusky window. It was a faculty that gave him much more a terrible sense of human abysses than a desire rashly to sound them and rise to the surface with his report. On the surface—the surface of the soul and the edge of the tragedy—he preferred to remain.... But of all cynics he was the brightest and kindest, and the subtleties he spun are mere silken threads for stringing polished beads. His collection of moral mysteries is the cabinet of a dilettante."

By the turn of the century, however, Hawthorne's mature reader would no longer feel old-romantic chills at the touch of the wizard hand. Neither would he, to justify old revolts, feel it necessary to deny the paternity of certain esthetic impulses. As represented by Lewis E. Gates, for instance, that reader would find nothing in Hawthorne to appall—beside the decadents, Hawthorne's reputed morbidity would seem quaintly wholesome. Only the art and the ideas were enticing to Gates. "Hawthorne is a master spinner of beautiful webs," Gates would write, "and the most rabid devotee of art for art's sake cannot well refuse to enjoy the fineness and consistency of his designs, the continuity and firmness of his texture, and the richness and depth of his tinting. ... But though Hawthorne dreams in terms of the ten commandments, ... for some of us who still believe that life is greater than art, his dreams are all the more fascinating artistically because they are deeply, darkly, beautifully true." Not just the date but the textures of criticism were moving into a new era when Gates could say:

> At present, Hawthorne is at a decided disadvantage, because, while remote enough to seem in trifles here and

there archaic, he is yet not remote enough to escape contemporary standards or to be read with imaginative historical allowances and sympathy, as Richardson or Defoe is read. Hawthorne's romances have the human quality and the artistic beauty that ensure survival; and in a generation or two, when the limitations of the Romantic ideal and the scope of Romantic methods have become historically clear in all men's minds, Hawthorne's novels will be read with an even surer sense than exists today of the imperfectness of equipment and occasional faults of manner that were the result of his environment and age.

Soon after the turn of the century there would come a rich revival of Hawthorne scholarship and criticism with the centenary of his birth in 1904. But by then figures like George Woodberry, William Peterfield Trent, and Paul Elmer More had come to maturity. Theirs would be a serious, Arnoldian view, heralding the Neo-Humanism of an imminent era and projecting Hawthorne toward the present Age of Criticism.

7 / The Howells Nobody Knows

NEVER WELL STUDIED, THE LITERARY REPUTATION OF W. D. Howells has a curious history. His work has been subjected to much demonstrably ignorant abuse, yet a wide spectrum of sensitive and significant readers have admired it. Mark Twain and Henry James were not only Howells's devoted friends, they were eloquent in testimony to his grace and insight. Taine, Turgenev, Tolstoi, Palacio Valdés, Björnson, and Bernard Shaw were numbered among his contemporary foreign admirers.

At Howells's death, Kipling said, "he is the father of a multitude of heirs who have inherited his treasures, but forgotten the paternity. Time will prove it so and your land's literature will acknowledge it." If that "beautiful time" for Howells which Henry James predicted is still to come, there is still reason to expect its arrival. Despite such irresponsibilities as Sinclair Lewis's Nobel Prize Speech, it is increasingly known that Hamlin Garland, Harold Frederic, Stephen Crane, and Booth Tarkington, in some of their best and most serious work were disciples of Howells. Van Wyck Brooks lived so to reverse his opinion that his last major book was a tribute, *Howells, His Life and World.* The dominant note of concern in the postwar era was struck by Lionel Trilling in 1951. He stressed the need of the contemporary mind to recover its lost ability to attend to the civility of Howells. Indeed, a common denominator among Howells's otherwise diverse admirers may be said to be concern for the grace, measure, social morality, and humanity, above all else for the *civilization* in a writer who uniquely engaged himself with civilization as an immediate, commonplace American phenomenon.

Apart from the growing recognition of Howells's intrinsic, expressive and artistic distinction, there can be no doubt of his historical importance. It is impossible to understand the development of the American novel, novella and short story, travel book, autobiography, sketch, essay, or, indeed, poetry without him. His contributions to literary theory, to practical criticism, and to literary vogue are of major import for the study of comparative as well as American literature. His memoirs constitute a class in themselves.

In spite of these facts, there are, it seems to me, five Howellses imperfectly known and crying for study. There is the master of the comic imagination championed by George Arms. Balancing him, there is the master of a distinctively realistic tragic vision, explored in my volumes and restudied by George Carrington. Then there is the surprisingly modern analyst of artistic loneliness and alienation, mostly unknown but hinted at by Richard Foster. There is the psychological novelist, almost completely unknown. And, finally, there is the permanent novelist, on whom George Bennett and Kermit Vanderbilt have worked, with his as yet imperfectly analyzed art and his distinctive dealings with Christianity, democracy, and the problem of selfhood. It is the fourth of these, the Howells that almost nobody knows, the psychological novelist, whom I wish to sketch.

I

PROBABLY THE BEST WAY TO APPROACH HOWELLS'S psychological fiction is to glance at what can be known about his personal psychological experience. We know that there was an abyssal split between his two earliest memories, dating from the springtime following his third birthday on March 1, 1840. That spring his family moved away from the tiny brick cottage in which he was born, and his memories were those stamped deep by farewell and transit. The child woke in the morning to gaze with absorptive wonder into the fecund beauty of a peach tree dense with bloom and lit by the early sun. "To me," said the grown author, "there is no blossom more pathetic or impassioned."

If peach blossoms meant exultation, abundance, security, and hope (among other things, no doubt), a paired memory meant the opposite. The mother with her tiny children traveled by steamboat from Wheeling, Virginia, to Cincinnati on their way to Hamilton, Ohio. Somewhere on the river the boat stopped. The child knelt on the window seat of the ladies' cabin in the stern, watching raindrops dance on the surface of the yellow water. The ship's yawl came into sight bearing a strange passenger, a one-legged man supporting himself with a crutch under one arm and a cane in his other hand. At the ship's side the man struggled to lunge aboard, missed his step, and vanished into the muddy river as silently and finally as the splashing drops of rain. Image of beauty and promise: image of terror and loss.

In themselves, those paired first memories prove only what his work proves anyway—that Howells was endowed with extraordinary sensibility. But they acquire a weighty symbolic value in the light of the rest of his life and his fiction. Robust and active though small, Howells as a boy responded to something, possibly family tensions, by living a secret life of vivid, awful nightmares. Awake he became the victim of obsessional superstitions and, upon occasion, unbearable homesickness. In adolescence his neuroses climaxed in a series of resounding nervous breakdowns with interesting, if pitiful, external symptoms. The worst of his childhood obsessions possessed the adolescent with a hypochondriacal delusion that he would at any moment break into the fatal agonies of rabies. Nostalgia defeated him repeatedly on the threshold of the journalistic success his brilliant abilities warranted him even as a teenager. If he tried to defy his symptoms they metamorphosized into prostrating vertigo.

Only a long, tough fight saved Howells. He was slowly helped by achievement, by growing newspaper success and cautiously cultivated literary success. His courage to gamble on spending four years in Venice four thousand miles from home and mother paid off brilliantly. And he became permanently established psychologically by the successful marriage contracted during his Venetian years.

But it is worth something to observe what prices Howells paid for his equilibrium—for the magnificent (perhaps compensatory) strength, balance, gentleness, empathetic sensitivity, and generosity for which his personality became famous. For years he was forced to stand with those seers-not of evil whom William James called "the healthy-minded." Like many another inward sufferer, Howells made his first reputation as a wit. His gaiety, fun, elegance, delicacy, satire, polish, and urbane goodness early delighted an international audience. They ignored the deeper levels of irony and blackness in his work. During the 1870's he enjoyed enviable interna-

141

tional success as a sort of Richard Steele *redivivus*. It must have been a real temptation to emulate Bret Harte and just go right on coining money and celebrity for doing the same thing over and over. It is of the essence of Howells's greatness that he refused merely to repeat. He insisted on growing, permitting his vision of life to deepen and darken, risking his audience and income repeatedly, until he ended at his ultimate psychological view.

Up to its first climax in the writing of Howells's pioneering realistic tragedy, *A Modern Instance,* his story has been told in detail (and, I think, with valuable differences in emphasis) in my and in Olov Fryckstedt's books. Three years after that point, Howells would experience the time during the latter stages of writing *The Rise of Silas Lapham* when, as he said, "the bottom dropped out." As nearly as one can tell, what he meant was that his defensive stock of peach-blossom optimism suddenly dropped toward zero. The effect of this might be compared to the moral significance of *The Rise of Silas Lapham.* (The perceptions lying behind that portrayal may, indeed, have knocked the bottom out.) Over the years, it seems to me, too many incautious critics have mistaken what is involved in the observations that *Lapham* is "optimistic" and "comic." It *is* both much as Dante's mighty masterpiece is both. The great difference in this respect is that where Dante's perspectives became cosmic, ultimately celestial, Howells's brand of realism confined his perspective to the worldly and humane. But the truest force of a realist's morality in *The Rise of Silas Lapham* bears upon Silas's repentance. His turning again at the price of pride and fortune wins him only the grace of a rise from the pit up to the plane of free humanity. His vision cleared, he may begin upon the good, humble life, once more a man. When the bottom dropped out for Howells, perhaps it let him down too from heights of thinking of himself more rosily than he ought.

Perhaps the psychic healing of the years then permitted Howells to afford a new sensitivity to social deprivation, suffering, frustration, and death in the new industrial society and so let him descend from healthy-mindedness. At any rate, he not only survived the succeeding years of black personal tragedy, he grew significantly into a new tragic vision. There came the slow dying of his lovely, gifted daughter, a terrible time exacerbated by medical bungling, by a primitive psychiatric ignorance in physicians which plunged Howells into the redoubled grief of his wife's psychic near-destruction. In the midst of that time came the moment when, in a little shack upon the mountainside above a sanatorium, he had to decide to stand, alone among the literary and public men of America, against the awful injustice done the Chicago Anarchists by a furious, hysterical nation. Soon after came the death of his daughter.

For weeks Howells was stunned. Then, in the summer of 1889, he was released into the most daimonic creative outpouring of his life. From that he achieved *A Hazard of New Fortunes*. And before he knew from the sensational national acceptance of his novel that it had not only saved him but elevated him to the status of leading American author, the Dean of American Letters, he was swept forward by the current of his creativity into the experimentalism of a psychological novel, *The Shadow of a Dream*, and then to the extraordinary (for that period) psychic confessions of *A Boy's Town*.

After that, Howells's writing was to be all more or less psychological. But his principal psychological fictions I should name, in order of composition, as *The Shadow of a Dream, An Imperative Duty, The Quality of Mercy, The Landlord at Lion's Head, The Son of Royal*

Langbrith, and *The Leatherwood God.* This is not to mention the sometimes probing short stories gathered in *A Pair of Patient Lovers, Questionable Shapes,* and *Between the Dark and the Daylight.*

I I

A HAZARD OF NEW FORTUNES ENDED ON A NOTE unusual for a realist. It was the business of the realist, Howells told Stephen Crane, to give people a true use of their eyes, to let them see clearly. But the final meditations of Basil March in *A Hazard* stress mysteries. There is the mystery of death itself, the mystery of suffering, and the mystery of atonement by suffering. There is the last mystery of character—what might one think of Margaret Vance, the Anglo-Catholic ministrant to the poor in the slums, who had romantically sent Conrad Dryfoos to his death but then joined a sisterhood and become apparently serene? It was in keeping with realism that Howells should refuse to pretend to "go behind" the visible into the recesses of Margaret's mind. The last line of the book is Basil's comment, "We must trust that look of hers." But it was not at all in keeping with standard realism that so much should be left impenetrable to the eye.

Howells swept on to his next book without apparent fatigue or pause after the mighty exertion of finishing *A Hazard.* This one became a brief, tight-knit work, experimental in form and concerned with dark, elusive questions available only to the inlooking eye of the psychological novelist. In dealing with the materials of *The Shadow of a Dream,* Howells would come to see that a whole theory of civilization, upon which he had for a fighting decade based his career and his faith in the supremacy of realism, was threatened. He was anticipating a fundamental part of the intellectual hisory of the twentieth century.

To concentrate on its psychological aspect, *The Shadow of a Dream* concerns a romantically self-indulgent man who uses the power of friendship and the terror of his coronary disease to hold his lovely wife Hermia and the oldest friend of his long bachelordom together in his household. This ménage-à-trois is technically innocent. The friend, James Nevil, is a brilliantly handsome Anglican priest who had first introduced and then married Faulkner to Hermia. Nevil and Hermia are demonstratively devoted to Faulkner—yet it is evident to Basil and Isabel March, Howells's recurrent team of sensitive observers, that a horribly obsessive dream which haunts Faulkner has eaten away his will to live and subjects him to coinciding paroxysms of hatred and *angina pectoris*. The dream, we learn toward the end of the book, was, in the words of Faulkner's mother, that Hermia and James "were—attached, and were waiting for him to die, so that they could get married. Then he would see them getting married in church, and at the same time it would be his funeral [Nevil, of course, officiating at both], and he would try to scream out that he was not dead; but Hermia would smile and say to the people that she had known James before she knew Douglas, and then *both* ceremonies would go on, and he would wake."

Howells provides evidence to suggest that he was aware of those implications of everybody's potential guilts and ambivalences all around the triangle to which our post-Freudian minds inevitably turn. As a pre-Freudian, however, Howells was interested in something else. Eventually the weight of the shadow of Faulkner's dream tragically destroyed all three people. Now the question became, was that because the dream had divinatory power? Faulkner had argued to Basil March that it must:

> "There's a whole region of experience—half the map of our life—that they tell us must always remain a wilderness, with all its extraordinary phenomena irredeemably savage and senseless. For my part, I don't believe it. I will put the wisdom of the ancients before the science of the moderns, and I will say with Elihu, 'In a dream, in a vision of the night, when deep sleep falleth upon men, in slumberings upon the bed; then He openeth the ears of men, and sealeth their instruction.' "
>
> "It's noble poetry," I said.
>
> "It's more than that," said Faulkner, "It's truth."

The ground of March's opposing logic is most interesting. Thought like Faulkner's, he urges, constitutes a "return to the bondage of the superstitions that cursed the childhood of the race . . . if I had a dream that contained a forecast or a warning of evil, I should feel it my duty in the interest of civilization to defy it. . . ."

March, and Faulkner's physician, Dr. Wingate, unite in holding that only the material, the empirically knowable, the scientifically measurable and logically controllable can be real to the civilized mind. Faulkner's dream they think mere insanity, the product no doubt of the disease that killed him. Wingate denies that the dream had anything to do with Faulkner's death. But nothing can convince Mrs. March, Hermia, or old Mrs. Faulkner of that; and March and Nevil are eventually shaken. At the end, as so often in Hawthorne—or Howells—, we are left not sure whether Faulkner's dream had divined a guilt so dark that neither his wife nor his friend could quite realize it. But we *are* made sure of some uncomfortable truths about "the mystery of human solidarity" in our necessity to share in the sorrow and suffering of the rest of mankind, even until solidarity comes to seem like

the Nemesis of Greek Tragedy, as the Marches twice remark. And we are made sure of realities not dreamt of in
Dr. Wingate's philosophy. For it becomes clear that, cog-
nitive power or no, empirical existence or no, the shadow
of Faulkner's dream has had the power to grip and blast
the lives of Nevil and Hermia, if only "through their own
morbid conscientiousness, their exaggerated sensibility," as March says in his "civilized" mood. The dream
did have psychological power—and therefore reality—
even for the Marches themselves.

Howells's personal conclusion was, as he said in an
enthusiastic review of William James's great *Principles
of Psychology* more than a year later, that psychology
formed an immensely important but largely mysterious
field "not yet explored or mapped except at a few points."
Even after all the mighty explorations since, it is noteworthy how true his comment remains that "the talk is
not only about, but round about the human mind, which
it penetrates here and there and wins a glimpse of unsay-
able things." But of course that condition served mainly
to stimulate Howells toward further reconnaissance of
the uses of the mystery in his own work.

He found exciting new uses almost at once in pioneering extensions of his social fiction. The first of these
occurred in *An Imperative Duty,* the race-problem and
miscegenation novel which followed next as fiction after
The Shadow of a Dream. When Sinclair Lewis began
research for *Kingsblood Royal* he was astonished to find
that the Howells he had ignorantly scorned in the '20's
had been the only writer to anticipate him in what he
felt, I think correctly, to be the heart of the matter. For
the "race problem" in the United States is not so much a
matter of color as it is of respect and self-respect—a psychological and moral problem of the exorcism of primitive, pagan superstitions and cruelly childish sentimen-

talities. The problems of the Negro in the South were not solved by translating them into his problems in the North. The core of the difficulty remained in the psychology of the situation for the Northerner, white or Negro. Howells's early insight into that fact gave *An Imperative Duty* a still current psychological and moral reality.

As in *The Shadow of a Dream,* Howells made this novel in form what Willa Cather would call a novel "démeublé," disfurnished, stripped to essentials. There are only three main characters, all just returned from residence and social acquaintanceship in Florence: Mrs. Meredith, a hyperconscientious and sentimental lady; her dramatically beautiful niece, Rhoda Aldgate; and Dr. Olney, a specialist in what Howells called "nerves" and we should call neuroses. Homesick for Italy, Olney finds the warmest, most vital people in Boston to be the Negroes who have increased so in numbers there since the Civil War. He finds that Rhoda has a like attraction toward them but that the *malaise* for which he is treating Mrs. Meredith is sharpened by race prejudice. As professional visits continue, Olney becomes increasingly enchanted by Rhoda. Then Mrs. Meredith confesses the source of her trouble: Rhoda is engaged to a blond, conventional Yankee clergyman; only Mrs. Meredith knows that Rhoda is genetically one-sixteenth black (by American standards still technically Negro). Mrs. Meredith is being shaken to pieces by the question of whether to tell Rhoda.

As Olney hears this, he learns something about the psychology of prejudice in "a turmoil of emotion for which there is no word but disgust. . . . His own race instinct expressed itself in a merciless rejection of her beauty, her innocence, her helplessness because of her race. The impulse had to have its course; and then he mastered it, with an abiding compassion, and a sort of

148

tender indignation." When, against Olney's advice, Mrs. Meredith does tell Rhoda, the girl's response rages through every level of terror, resentment, self-pity and self-hatred. Poor sentimental Mrs. Meredith commits suicide while Rhoda ranges distraughtly through the Negro section, fearing and hating the black skins, the Negroid features, yet jealous because they have always known of themselves what is catastrophically ravaging her.

Howells suggests remedies for this tragically wicked psychological nonsense by letting Rhoda learn two things. One is moral, as she hears a young divinity student preach in a Negro church: "oh, if our white brethren could only understand . . . that if they would help us a little more they needn't hate us so . . . I believe it's the only way out of all the trouble in the world. You can't fight your way out, and you can't steal your way out, and you can't lie your way out. But you can *love* your way out. . . . By helpin' somebody else!" The other is intellectual. Knowing more than she thinks, Olney can lay siege to Rhoda with full intelligence. When he proposes, she seems for a fraction of a second to accede, then leaps to her feet to gasp, "Never! I am a Negress!" But he has come better rehearsed than she. He smiles, persuades, laughs at her confusion, and wins. The point is that a lot of romantic sentimentality about race and miscegenation needs mere deflation. And so it does.

Positively, however, the point Howells is making here is the same as that in his next three major psychological novels. It is a blend of psychological with ethical insight which constitutes the ultimate vision of this later, unknown Howells. In a proposal to S.S. McClure to write what became *The Quality of Mercy*, Howells made a comment which reveals how thoroughly psychological his artistic intention had become. His earlier realism would have been by definition as true to objective evidences as possible. But now he says, "The whole design shows fantastic in some points, but I believe it to be thoroughly realistic, in the deep, interior way, where I should seek my strongest dramatic effects, while on the surface I should try to keep a constant play of incident for those who could not look below it." This interior study of an embezzling business man who flees to Canada concentrates thematically and symbolically as well as psychologically on the experience of the defalcator. What Northwick, accustomed to success, power, luxury, gradually discovers is that an arrogant life has emptied him of inward reality. Stripped of possessions, he does not really exist but walks the world a kind of golem or zombie. Only as love and grief for his deserted daughters build up in his heart can he acquire reality. And with that comes a longing for return and expiation. He sends for an American detective, crosses the border in handcuffs—"I want the atonement to begin as soon as possible," he says—and drops dead. "Sometimes I think there *was* nothing to Northwick, except what happened to him," says an observer.

So much for the business man as mere pirate. But how about the society which produced him? Was it responsible? Did it so frame the conditions of success as to create the fierce emptiness, the essential nonbeing of the successful man? Howells was asking such questions at the end of *The Quality of Mercy.* He did not answer them until *The Landlord at Lion's Head,* 1897. This was to be a novel anything but *démeublé.* Howells furnished it from an experience of summer hotels, as he said, "extending over a quarter of a century, and scarcely to be surpassed if paralleled." He added the fruits of a thirty years' observation of the social hierarchies of Harvard College. And he capped it with the prizes of the only thorough, masculine investigation of the life of New England made during the last third of the nineteenth century. Seeking, as he said, "a true rustic New England type in contact with urban life under entirely modern conditions," and a realization of "that anti-Puritan quality which was always vexing the heart of Puritanism," Howells found him in the nearly picaresque hero of the book, Jeff Durgin. Jeff voyages vertically through the levels of American society. Sanguine, energetic, aggressive, and sensual among his pale, phthisic, and conscientious relatives, Jeff is a pure "natural man"—a "comical devil" always in trouble, a charming *bon vivant* born to "keep hotel," and a defiant rebel against any "stress put upon him for righteousness." From his birth in the back Yankee hills amid decadence, squalor, and defeat, what hope could there be for this rugged young savage? Economically he and his mother discover the way out through summer people. Step by step they move from the farm house with a boarding painter to keeping a boarding house to running a summer hotel. But as the visiting world becomes less Arcadian and more Society with rising affluence, Jeff discovers the essentials of the world's worldliness: money, social position, fashion; being In or Out. The instincts of Society are revealed to be as savage as his own. He goes to Harvard and finds more of the same. Exploiting Harvard contacts, he gains entrée to Proper Boston and finds still more of the same. He learns that, "Prosperity and adversity, they've nothing to do with conduct. If you're a strong man, you get there, and if you're a weak man, all the righteousness in the universe won't help you ... I shall be blessed if I look out for myself; and if I don't I shall suffer for my want of foresight."

Jeff learns foresight. He marries for social position. He makes a crashing resort success out of Lion's Head

Hotel on the site of the family farm (with a handy fire to help out). He becomes a "gentleman," one of the international set. But has he been "blessed"? The psychology of power, what John Woolman had called the Spirit of Fierceness, succeeds. Howells let the painter Westover, the novel's "register" who has watched Jeff from boyhood, comment: "Jeff Durgin sowed success in a certain way, and he's reaping it. He once said to me, when I tried to waken his conscience, that he should get where he was trying to go if he was strong enough, and being good had nothing to do with it. I believe now he was right. But he was wrong, too, as such a man always is. That kind of tree bears Dead Sea apples, after all. He sowed evil, and he must reap evil. He may never know it, but he will reap what he has sown. The dreadful thing is that others must share in his harvest."

Readers who had any serious doubts about the truth of this could refer back to the fate of Northwick, or to that of Jacob Dryfoos in *A Hazard of New Fortunes*. The shocking implication was that the structure of American society awards success almost automatically to the psychology of the anti-Puritan "natural man," the ruthless, amoral savage.

But of course the psychology of power was not limited in scope to economics or social climbing. And it was in following it beyond those long-time concerns that Howells produced the most unpredictable of his psychological fictions in *The Son of Royal Langbrith*, 1904. In various ways this is among the most fascinating of Howells's novels. In it he answers as well as he ever could that "riddle of the painful earth" which he had asked so frequently since *The Rise of Silas Lapham*. He faced the problem of the "Dead Sea apples" planted by a dead father's evil to set the teeth of his son on edge. And he was able to do that only by departing wholly from accustomed themes to cultivate the germ of an idea held in the back of his mind for at least fifteen years. "Filial Love," reads an earlier notebook entry. "Son who prevents his mother's second marriage." By the time Howells got ready to look for a title, he would describe the work as "the story of an evil so long concealed that it is best for all the injured it should never be known. . . ." He thought of titles like *Reconciliation* or *The Law of Limitation*. He played with the suggestions of a proverb he knew as Tuscan: *"Iddio non paga sabato"*—"God does not pay on Saturdays"—with its unspoken answer—*"ma paga"*—"but He pays!" All of those implied the novel's retort upon the problem of evil. But the title finally chosen emphasized surprising news: Howells had somehow grasped his own concept of what Freud was soon to make famous as the Oedipus complex.

In the opening scene of the novel, Dr. Justin Anther and Mrs. Amelia Langbrith confront the fact that she is too weak to accept his proposal of marriage. She has been left widowed for nineteen years by a bigamous, sadistic scoundrel of a husband, and she loves Anther. But she cannot break the sentimental tyranny of her son. James Langbrith, never told the truth, has invented a sublime father-image. His mother cannot escape from servitude to her son's worship of that false god. She has no courage to tell him the truth. She and Anther, and indeed the whole town of Saxmills, dominated by the Langbrith paper mill, are forced to pay homage to the patronizing pride of the filial devotion of the son of Royal Langbrith. The worst of the other sufferers are James's uncle John Langbrith, whose generation of silence about Royal has given him ulcers, and Hawberk, the laudanum-drinker, from whom Royal Langbrith had stolen an invention which made his paper mill successful.

The heritage of Langbrith's evil broods over Saxmills. And surely the son's arrogant, impious piety should provoke Nemesis if ever *hubris* did. Howells had plotted redemption, not "cheap tragedy," for James, however; and he took pains to give James redeeming qualities different from "the outright brute Jeff Durgin was." He let James fall in love with Hawberk's daughter Hope and tell her and be loved in return before he discovered his mother's affection for Anther. Then, though James choked with rage at this betrayal and desecration of his Father and tried to find words "to hurt Anther to death, so far as insult could kill; and . . . to wither his mother with shame," his "blows . . . seemed to fall like blows dealt in nightmare, as if they were dealt with balls of cotton or down. . . ." Hope persuaded him not to break irrevocably with his mother but to take a promised year to study playwriting in Paris and let things settle.

James's absence left the poor victims of Royal Langbrith's malice in Saxmills to ponder the riddle of earth's pain, or evil. Though they all suffered as though Langbrith's diabolism were potent over time, death, and the grave, they were forced to agree that the good of the community and the future of the young lovers conspired against exposing the buried scoundrel. When Anther cures Hawberk, the lucid inventor concurs: "You might almost say that devil had planned it out to have his boy make it up with my girl, so as to stop my mouth for good and all." Two arguments arise against this Manicheism, both tentative. Perhaps, as for Anther the man of science, "the law that we find at work in the material world is, apparently, absent from the moral world; not . . . because it is without law, but because the law is of such cosmical vastness in its operation that it is only once or twice sensible to any man's experience." That is a possibility of faith. Otherwise, "so far as the sages or the saints are able convincingly to affirm, they have only the capricious vicissitudes of weather." Equally dark to the understanding is a Christian view urged by the local rector, the Reverend Mr. Enderby. Justice ultimately exceeds the grasp of man's mind. Men who "press for judgement . . . are in danger of becoming executioners." Man has therefore "a duty of mercy," leaving justice to God.

When James Langbrith returns home it is to horror-struck reality. Meeting his exasperated Uncle John on a train, he is told the truth, which seemed "to rage upon him like some war of the elements, and he was aware not only of the truth of what had been told him, but of its not being novel. He had that mystic sense of its all having happened before, long ago, and of a privity to it, in his inmost, dating back to his first consciousness." But there is little he can do. Hawberk has died in a mill accident, and just as James arrives Anther dies of an infection caught from a patient. James's first impulse is the romantic one to psychic suicide, to renounce Hope and expose himself and his father to the public. But Hope and Enderby succeed in holding him to reality. His best penance will be to live quietly with himself and the truth, Enderby tells him. And this he manages to do, making a happy marriage out of an enlightened humiliation.

What, then, of the problem of evil? Did Royal Langbrith get away with it? Enderby, speaking Howells's most audacious guess at the riddle of the painful earth, thinks not. "Could there be fearfuler suffering," he asks, than Royal Langbrith's "consciousness in his sudden death that he could not undo here the evil he had done?" And then, with whatever hedging enforced by Mrs. Enderby's Puritan reluctance, Enderby, in almost the last words of the novel, asks, "How do we know but that in the mystical legislation, as to whose application to our conduct we have to make our guesses and inferences, there may not be a law of limitations by which the debts overdue through time are the same as forgiven? No one was the poorer through their non-payment in Royal Langbrith's case; in every higher sort each was the richer. It may be the complicity of all mortal beings is such that the pain he inflicted was endured to his behoof, and that it has helped him atone for his sins as an acceptable offering in the sort of vicarious atonement which has always been in the world."

Howells's religious heritage was compounded of a strange set of radical views almost all largely heretical from the viewpoint of Christian orthodoxy. It was Quaker, Methodist, Millerite, Deistic, Swedenborgian, and Utopian. He had mixed in a leaven of agnosticism and then a charge of Tolstoi. Yet for years he had been unexplainedly fascinated by Anglo-Catholicism. His psychological fiction, like all his other fiction, had eventuated in ethical insight—and now at the end in religious concerns he frankly called "mystical" while he knew they were vaguely Christian. Evil is malevolence grown from egotism, and it ends in a horror of nothingness, of nonbeing. It breeds more evil in a competitive, soul-gambling world of chance and always more suffering. But in suffering there is hope. It may turn us to love and to the power to suffer with and for each other, to realize our complicity and eventually our solidarity with all men. In a more sophisticated way, Howells's last insights are not unlike Hawthorne's.

He could not reconcile his faith with what he thought the antique failures and conformities to a wicked world of every church. And it was in part to that dilemma that he devoted his late-blooming study, *The Leatherwood God*. Here, conscious of the shadows of age closing upon his energies, Howells used his last chance and triumphantly solved a problem that had baffled him since the age of seventeen—how to write an effective novel about the backwoods Ohio of his father's period. He chose a complex topic. Back in the actual history of frontier Ohio, a fanatic had convinced residents of Leatherwood Creek that he was God. Howells frankly based his outline on published history: "The drama is that of the actual events in its main development," he acknowledged. "But the vital incidents, or the vital use of them, are the author's." He took particular pains to emphasize that "the characters are all invented as to their psychological evolution. . . ." What, he was asking himself, in other words, could be the human meaning of the rise, triumph, and catastrophe of the Leatherwood God?

There is no room here to admire in this novel the vividness and dramatic force of some of the most picturesque scenes Howells ever wrote. We shall have to concentrate on the psychological perspectives. The reader always sees Dylks, the false prophet, dramatically —from the outside, that is. Howells shows us how confused Dylks himself was by the weird cloud of self-deceit, superstition, and rascality with which he surrounded himself. The terrible pathos of his situation appeared when he had duped his "Little Flock" of followers into serving his egotism and then discovered that he had become the slave of theirs. *And* they expected miracles. Half believing in himself, he advertises a miracle, it fails, and he nearly undergoes martyrdom. But Dylks shrinks from the ultimate weapon of the prophets; he hasn't the stomach either to fight or be martyred.

The sensitive observer or "register," and in some ways the *raisonneur,* of the novel is the village freethinker and rationalist, Squire Braile. It is he who saves Dylks from lynching. Refusing to play Pilate to Dylks's brassy parody of the Passion of Christ, Braile turns Dylks into a frontier joke. He will neither permit a lynching nor, as Justice of the Peace, railroad the prophet. Under the laws of Ohio, he points out, freedom of worship is guaranteed: "Now, then, have you folks got any other charge against him? Has he stolen anything? Like a mule, for instance? Has he robbed a hen-roost? Has he assaulted anybody? or set a tobacco-shed on fire? Some one must make a charge; I don't much care what it is."

When nothing concrete comes forth, Braile lets the prophet race into the woods and tells the "Little Flock" and their antagonists, "The Herd of the Lost," as Dylks had named friend and foe, "Now, you fellows, both sides, go home, and look after your corn and tobacco; and you women, you go and get breakfast for them, and wash up your children and leave the Kingdom of Heaven alone for a while." As the mob shuffles uneasily, he turns on the persecutors: "And you . . . you let these folks worship any stock or stone they've a mind to; and you find out the true God if you can, and stick to Him, and don't bother the idolators. I reckon He can take care of Himself. I command you to disperse. Go home! Get Out! Put!"

There is a finally dominant note here of the silvery laughter of the mind. But it rules over much that is bitter and black. *The Leatherwood God* is a tragicomedy. There is the tragedy of the awful entrapment of Dylks, who discovers that when he has been saved from the "Herd of the Lost" he dare not tell the truth to the "Little Flock." They would kill him if he should. And he wanders off at last with the remnant toward Philadelphia hoping something will turn up. When it doesn't, he lets himself slip into a river and be drowned.

Still worse, there are the tragedies of the people close to Dylks, his abused wife and her family. There are the terrible tensions on those who are converted—and those who are not. In part, observers judge that Dylks's spell over the others is ordinary: "He just gave them the *chance* to play the fool," says a Calvinist. Obviously the one strong temptation is love of status, especially in the local businessmen. They buy and bully their way into discipleships, the two richest becoming St. Peter and St. Paul.

But Howells's suggested explanation for the basic power of the Leatherwood God would have surprised his critics, particularly of the 1920's, if they had troubled to read before they wrote. Like any other country boy, Howells was aware of the mighty sexual stimuli which peopled the brush surrounding a successful camp meeting with coupling forms. Mark Twain had commented that his devoutly Presbyterian mother was too sensible to let him go to revivals. Talking his novel over with S. Weir Mitchell, novelist and foremost American psychotherapist, Howells had hinted at "some tremendous things," and Mitchell had begged him to go on with "that final and too daring novel. . . ." Some things, Howells answered, he could treat indirectly. Those, "I can perhaps help the reader to imagine for me, if I can't do it for him," he said.

The hidden topic obviously is s— E x. Equally obviously, no one ought to rush out to get *The Leatherwood God* if he is interested in the psychologically unimaginable physiological sprees which pass for representations of human sexuality in current romance. Howells customarily argued, finally too rigidly, for a sane, responsible reticence in fictional reference to sex. Ethically and socially, to say nothing of artistically, present writers are making him appear far more attractive in that stance than he seemed forty years ago.

Nevertheless, it was simply not true, though Ludwig Lewisohn said it, that Howells went into "a negative frenzy" at the mere notion of sex. Mitchell is said to have thrown his first copy of a volume of Freud into the fireplace. But Howells did not hesitate to make it clear that the root of Leatherwood Creek's delusion lay in the *mana,* the charismatic attraction of Dylks—and that that magnetism was sexual. Howells said it artistically, not intrusively but unmistakably. Repeatedly the text emphasizes Dylks's tall, mysterious, handsome figure with its black, tossing, gleaming mane of hair and his great shout "Salvation!" followed by an extraordinary equine snort. In meetings hysterical women grovel at his feet. Matthew Braile reflects, "This god of theirs is a handsome devil and some poor fool of a girl, or some bigger fool of a married woman, is going to fall in love with him, and then—"

"Did you just think of that?" says Mrs. Braile.

Blackmailing his real wife into silence, Dylks tries to seduce her niece into becoming an Egyptian dual deity with him. But David Gillespie defies him: "You—you turkey cock, you stallion! But you can't prance *me* down. . . ." It is desecration of his stallion's mane by the Herd of the Lost, who tear out a handful, scalp and all, for Jane Gillespie's sake, which initiates the destruction of Dylks. The point is clear, and it provides the *motif* for the entire "psychological evolution" of the "vital" factors in the book up to the triumph and the bathos of Dylks's victory and disgrace and down to the anticlimax of release and good riddance dominating the pathos of his death in Howells's frontier tragicomedy.

The best of what Howells wrote in the twentieth century was neither untypical nor unworthy of it. And when one asks how the American literature of this century came to be what it has become, he can find some of the answers in the late career of that surprisingly contemporaneous author, a psychological novelist pioneering up almost to his end a fifth of the way into the century, the Howells nobody knows.

8 / Howells and Crane:

Violence, Decorum and Reality

THE CURRENTLY POPULAR ASSERTION THAT VIOLENCE IS somehow distinctively or peculiarly American is easy to refute by historical, etiological reference. In the springtime of the Jamestown Colony, for instance, they punished one of the lads by escorting him out into the forest and nailing his hand with a dagger so firmly to a tree that whenever he should decide to come home he would have to use the blade to cut through his hand and free himself. When the Pilgrim Fathers found that Thomas Morton was cultivating love, joy and good Indian relations over at Merry Mount they despatched Miles Standish with his squad of citizen soldiers to put a stop not only to sin but Merry Mount.

Such actions of the national dawn were not, however, in the least "American." They were European and not even close to the worst acts of physical and psychic repression Europeans regularly practiced upon each other at home and upon other peoples abroad. Colonial atrocities in the area of what was to become the United States were rather average on a European scale. And, of course, there was nothing extraordinary about European cruelty and repression. If anything, they were less refined than those practiced in certain more advanced countries of Asia. Cruelty and repression seemed universal, seemed inescapable in the human condition; they seemed "human."

What is more interesting than the violence, really, is that there developed strong American variants upon those traditions of antiviolence which had begun to arise from such sources as St. Francis, Erasmus, George Fox, Herbert of Cherbury, and Voltaire. There were, and are, powerful intellectual currents, and sensibilities, and life-styles set against violence, and set to promote peace and reconciliation, which are at least as "American" as violence. Quakers, Mennonites, the Amish, and other pacifists flocking to the new world, the deist-democrats whose minds and writings dominated the founding of the republic, the utopians springing up in every generation, the romantic idealists—all carried historic testimonies against violence with substantial effects both in this country and beyond.

When one comes to think of it, all of the foregoing is well known. What seems hardly to be known at all is that the disillusioned successors of Whitman and Thoreau, the realists and agnostics who stand in many ways closer to our spiritual condition than the transcendentalists, also spoke to the issue of American violence. Therefore it seems worth while to attend to those aspects of the art of Howells and of Stephen Crane which can be summed up under the rubric of "Violence, Decorum, and Reality." They speak significantly to our present condition, not shutting their eyes to the facts of human violence but esthetically portraying their vision of the right way to see it and to deal with it, especially in our own minds. They suggest, on the whole, that violence is most dangerous when it becomes a disease of the imagination.

I

CONTRARY TO THE OPINION FORMERLY EXPRESSED BY ignorant and inadvertent critics (myself included), it is simply not true that violence is absent from the fiction of Howells. It is definitely, if not frequently, there. But what is finally interesting about the violence in Howells is the decorum with which his total commitment to realism compelled him to treat the violences of human reality. Though for a Howells novel an unusual amount of violence appears in *A Hazard of New Fortunes,* something, if not enough, has been said about it by critics; and it might be more profitable to look at examples from later work. Here is a scene from a turn of the century novel, *The Kentons.* It comes right in the middle of the book. A man called Bittridge has been playing fast and loose with the emotions of Judge Kenton's daughter Ellen, has followed the family to New York and assaulted and insulted the elderly Judge because he would not permit Bittridge to see Ellen again. Ladies of the family have written home to report. And so, when Bittridge gets off the train, he is met at the station by the family's eldest son, Richard Kenton:

> Bittridge, with his overcoat hanging on his arm, advanced towards [Richard] with the rest, and continued to advance, in a sort of fascination, after his neighbors, with the instinct that something was about to happen, parted on either side of Richard and left the two men confronted. Richard did not speak, but deliberately reached out his left hand, which he caught securely into Bittridge's collar; then he began to beat him with the cowhide wherever he could strike his writhing and twisting shape. Neither uttered a word, and except for the whir of the cowhide in the air, and the rasping sound of its arrest upon the body of Bittridge, the thing was done in perfect silence. The witnesses stood

well in the back in a daze, from which they recovered when Richard released Bittridge with a twist of the hand that tore his collar loose and left his cravat dangling, and tossed the frayed cowhide away, and turned and walked homeward. Then one of them picked up Bittridge's hat and set it aslant on his head, and others helped pull his collar together and tie his cravat.

For the few moments that Richard Kenton remained in sight they scarcely found words coherent enough for question and when they did, Bittridge had nothing but confused answers to give to the effect that he did not know what it meant, but he would find out. . . .

In his own house Richard Kenton lay down awhile, deadly sick, and his wife had to bring him brandy before he could control his nerves sufficiently to speak. Then he told her what he had done, and why, and Mary pulled off his shoes and put a hot-water bottle to his cold feet. It was not exactly the treatment for a champion, but Mary Kenton was not thinking of that, and when Richard said he still felt a little sick at the stomach she wanted him to try a drop of camphor in addition to the brandy.

The important thing is to see how carefully Howells has undercut his violence. It has been honestly presented but ironically undercut and limited. The method bespeaks a felt and philosophic sense of decorum regarding violence.

Another central case in point comes from one of the best but least known of Howells's books. Really his last novel, *The Leatherwood God* deals with the frontier of his parents' childhood. Historically there had appeared in Leatherwood Creek, Ohio, a prophet in its frontier religious life who convinced some townspeople that he was God—the Leatherwood God. As this scene opens, Joseph Dylks, the Leatherwood God, has failed to bring off a miracle he had proposed to exhibit publicly, and a mob of opponents, "the Hounds," closes in upon "the Little Flock." They break into the house:

In a circle of his worshipers, kneeling at his feet, stood Dylks, while they hailed him as their God and entreated his mercy. At the scramble behind them, they sprang up and stood dazed, confronting their enemies.

"We want Dylks! We want the Good Old Man! We want the Lion of Judah! Out of the way, Little Flock!" came in many voices; but when the worshipers yielded, Dylks had vanished.

A moment of awe spread to their adversaries, but in another moment the riot began again. The unbelievers caught the spirit of the worse among them and stormed through the house, searching it everywhere, from the cellar to the garret. A yell rose from them when they found Dylks half way up the chimney of the kitchen. His captors pulled him forward into the light, and held him cowering under the cries of "Kill him!" "Tie him to a tree and whip him!" "Tar and feather him!" "Ride him on a rail!"

"No, don't hurt him!" Redfield commanded. "Take him to a justice of the peace and try him."

"Yes," the leader of the Hounds assented. "Take him to Squire Braile. He'll settle with him."

The Little Flock rallied to the rescue, and some of the Herd joined them. As an independent neutral, Abel Reverdy, whom his wife stirred to action, caught up a stool and joined the defenders.

"Why, you fool," a leader of the Hounds derided him amiably, "what you want to do with that stool? If the Almighty can't help himself, you think *you're* goin' to help him?"

Abel was daunted by the reasoning, and even Sally stayed her war cries.

"Well, I guess there's sumpin' *in* that," Abel assented, and he lowered his weapon.

The incident distracted his captors and Dylks broke from them, and ran into the yard before the house. He was covered with soot and dust and his clothes were torn; his coat was stripped in tatters, and his long hair hung loose over it.

His prophecies of doom to those who should lay hands upon him had been falsified, but to the literal sense of David Gillespie he had not yet been sufficiently proved an impostor: till he should bring his daughter a strand of the hair which Dylks had proclaimed it death to touch, she would believe in him, and David followed in the crowd straining forward to reach Redfield, who with one of his friends had Dylks under his protection. The old man threw himself upon Dylks and caught a thick strand of his hair, dragging him backward by it. Redfield looked round. He said, "You want that, do you? Well I promised." He tore it from the scalp, and gave it into David's hand, and David walked back with it into the house where his daughter remained with the wailing and sobbing women-worshipers of the outraged idol.

He flung the lock at her feet. "There's the hair that it was death to touch." She did not speak; she only looked at it with horror.

"Don't you believe it's *his?*" her father roared.

"Yes, yes! I know it's his; and now let's go home and pray for him, and for *you,* father. We've both got the same God, now."

A bitter retort came to the old man's lips, but the abhorrent look of his daughter stayed his words, and they went into the night together, while the noise of the mob stormed back to them through the darkness, farther and farther away.

I I

VIOLENCE TREATED WITH THE FOREGOING SORT OF REductive decorum lacks commercial moxie. It is not "entertaining" in any fashion known to be popular. It won't "sell" because it suggests the opposites of superhumanism and escape. It is the violence of serious art, not of the entertainment industry. It was deliberately designed to counter what Howells called "effectism" and "the romanticistic."

In his *Harper's Monthly* column called "The Editor's Study" Howells during the winter of 1887–88 approached the peak of his role in the Realism War. The November column pounced on a happy saying in *The Renaissance in Italy* by John Addington Symonds. Speculating on whether art criticism might ever cleanse itself of the corruptions of mere fashionableness, Symonds had glimpsed a Darwinian hope that, in Howells's words,

> . . . in proportion as we gain a firmer hold upon our own place in the world, we shall come to comprehend with more instinctive certitude what is simple, natural, and honest. . . . The perception of the enlightened man will then be the taste of a healthy person who has made himself acquainted with the laws of evolution in art and in society, and is able to test the excellence of work in any stage from immaturity to decadence by discerning what there is of truth, sincerity, and natural vigor in it.

Reflection upon Symonds led Howells the next month to a brilliant expression of his own ideal. He summarized Symonds as having said that "what is unpretentious and what is true is enduringly beautiful and good, and nothing else is so." Then, lightly but carefully, he proceeded to quote Edmund Burke's *Essay on the Sublime and the Beautiful:* ignore art-traditions, never mind critics (they are often foolish):

> "The true standard of the artist is in every man's power" already, as Burke says; Michelangelo's "light of the piazza," the glance of the common eye, is and always was the best light on a statue; Goethe's "boys and blackbirds" have in all ages been the real connoisseurs of berries; but hitherto the mass of common men have been afraid to apply their own simplicity, naturalness, and honesty to the appreciation of the beautiful.

In fact, Howells was tracking in his sights bigger game than he was willing to startle before he got off his shot. Not so much truly the idealists as the genteel, petrified idealizers; not so much the Old Romantics as the new "romanticists," the neoromantics (*schlockmeister* was unfortunately not a word known to Howells) were his quarry. Threatened by realism, the idealizers and romanticists were harking back to the medieval moment when Realist meant Idealist. They threatened to succeed in pasting the labels of infidel, atheist, vulgarian, dullard, and mucker on the realists.

Howells's move to outflank them became a brilliant improvisation on a theme from Taine. "The young writer who attempts to report the phrase and carriage of everyday life, who tries to tell just how he has heard men talk and seen them look, is made to feel guilty of something low and unworthy," Howells complained, ". . . he is instructed to idealize his personages . . . in the spirit of wretched pedantry. . . ." Fulfilling his "mission to represent the petrification of taste," the wretched pedant would say to a young writer as he would say, given the chance, with the same confidence to a scientist:

> 'I see that you are looking at a grasshopper there that you have found in the grass, and I suppose you intend to describe it. Now don't waste your time and sin against culture in *that* way. I've got a grasshopper here, which has been evolved at considerable pains and expense out of the grasshopper in general; in fact, it's a type. It's made up of wire and card-board, very prettily painted in a conventional tint, and it's perfectly indestructible. It isn't very much like a real grasshopper, but it's a great deal nicer, and it's served to represent the notion of a grasshopper ever since man emerged from barbarism. You may say that it's artificial. Well, it *is* artificial: but then it's ideal too; and what you want to do is to cultivate the ideal. You'll find the books full of my kind of grasshopper, and scarcely a trace of yours in any of them. The thing that you are proposing to do is commonplace; but if you say that it isn't commonplace for the very reason that it hasn't been done before, you'll have to admit that it's photographic.'

However much, Howells went on, one might wish "the common, average man" would find the courage to "reject the ideal grasshopper," he must admit that it will not be at once: "the people who have been brought up on the ideal grasshopper, the heroic grasshopper, the impassioned grasshopper, the self-devoted, adventureful, good old romantic cardboard grasshopper, must die out before the simple, honest and natural grasshopper can have a fair field."

But Howells's perhaps finest critical moment was to be occasioned by the preface to *La Hermana San Sulpicio* of his friend the Spanish realist Armando Palacio Valdés. Howells began the November 1889 "Editor's Study" by musing about the decline of English fiction since Jane Austen: "With her example before them, why should not English novelists have gone on writing simply, honestly, artistically, ever after?" It is, he confessed, hard to be simple and honest. But he referred the question to Señor Valdés and his new preface. First he quoted Valdés's condemnation of French naturalism, disagreeing in part. "French naturalism is better at its worst than French unnaturalism at its best," said dry Howells. But then he turned to bring out the Valdés idea that all in nature is equal, and it is the business of the artist to catch, in his spirit, the beautiful effect which springs from true perception. "We may add," said Howells, "that there is no joy in art except this perception of the meaning of things and its communication; when you have felt it and told it . . . you have fulfilled the purpose for which you were born an artist."

Howells crowed approval of the insistence of Valdés that the only sin of the artist is to falsify and imitate. So long as he reports his true experience, all's well: " 'It is entirely false,' " said Howells's translation, " 'that the great romantic, symbolic, or classic poets modified nature; such as they expressed her they felt her; and in this view they are as much realists as ourselves. . . . Only those falsify her who, without feeling classic wise or romantic wise, set about being classic or romantic, wearisomely reproducing the models of former ages. . . .' " Agreeing, Howells added that he thought the "pseudo-realists" worst of all, "for they sin against the living; whereas those who continue to celebrate the heroic adventures of Puss in Boots and the hair-breadth escapes of Tom Thumb, under various aliases, only cast disrespect upon the immortals, who have passed beyond these noises."

For Howells, finally, the most telling point made by Valdés came from his saying, " 'The principal cause of the decadence of contemporary literature is found, in my thinking, in the vice which has been very graphically called *effectism,* or the itch of awaking at all cost in the reader vivid and violent emotions, which shall do credit to the invention and originality of the writer.' " *There,* Howells implied, lies our answer. The real culprits are the English critics: "From the point of view of modern English criticism, which likes to be melted, and hor- rified, and astonished, and blood-curdled, and goose- fleshed, no less than to be 'chippered up' in fiction, Señor Valdés were indeed incorrigible."

In the dominant world of popular taste, Howells agreed, effectism reigns. Like Feuillet or Bulwer or Dumas, "Dickens is full of it." But if "the *effectists* who delight genteel people at all the theatres, and in all the romances" will not satisfy Valdés, "what, we ask, will satisfy this extremely difficult Spanish gentleman?" Humanity? "simple, life-like character"? This, Howells remarked, "seems to us the cruelest irony, the most sar- castic affectation of humility. If you had asked that char- acter in fiction be superhuman, or subhuman, or pre- terhuman, or intrahuman, and had bidden the novelist go, not to humanity, but the humanities, for the proof of his excellence, it would have been all very easy."

The secret in the end, then, turns out to be that a perverse criticism has prevented the English from recovering from "the mania of romanticism . . . because English criticism, in the presence of the Continental masterpieces, has continued provincial and special and personal. . . ." Jane Austen was great because her honesty made her a realist in effect. "Realism is nothing more and nothing less than the truthful treatment of material, and Jane Austen was the first and the last of the English novelists to treat material with entire truthfulness. Because she did this, she remains the most artistic of the English novelists and alone worthy to be matched with the great Scandinavian and Slavic and Latin artists."

In general, historically the difference between a romantic and a neoromantic was that a romantic seriously believed romantic ideas; he had a genuine romantic faith. A neoromantic, who did not, could not, believe in romanticism, or romantic ideas, still thirsted for romantic effects. His was the error of "effectism." Some neoromantics were frank. Literature, they believed, existed to provide escape. Romantic effects provide good escape. Therefore it is the business of the writer to provide romantic effects even when he has no belief in their original grounds.

There is a letter, which has long fascinated me, which came about December 1, 1895, to Howells from Frederic Remington. Howells had published a favorable review of Owen Wister's book called *Red Men and White*, having known Wister for years and shared, like Henry James, substantial admiration for the man and his artistry. Remington, a friend of Wister's own generation, was a writer, painter, and sculptor of cowboy and Indian scenes —the man who rendered horses and Western action so superbly that we have continued to romanticize the West through his eyes. In that character he wrote Howells a sarcastically complimentary note boiling with half-suppressed fury:

> I have just got through with reading your "Life and Letters" [Howells's column] on Wister—For one who protests so much ignorance you come more nearly telling just what Wister is doing ("TRUTH"—) than any other fellow who is set in judgment on things of the sort. Wister is a great man and it gives me comfort to know that he will help me by his success to make people see *the thing* which is my soul. When one thinks that when I drew 'scouts—soldiers—injuns'—it was the worst of form to treat such 'red eyed' red covered—unreal stuff—it gives me courage to have you think Wister will finally bring home to such as you—*the thing*—the truth—however much you may not care for it. I wish that this had happened before Thanksgiving.

The bombast, the irony hardly masking contempt, of Remington's tough talk was competitively warranted by the ongoing victory of the neoromantics. For the public imagination, however, that victory was to become a disaster.

The difference between Howells's truth and Remington's shows up in the central moment of violence in Wister's *The Virginian*. Here is the *locus classicus* of the neoromantic, the effectist, portrayal of violence. A minor character in *The Virginian* is "the lost dog" called Shorty. Improvident and stupid in human relationships, he has only one treasure in life—his horse Pedro. Shorty is cajoled into selling his horse to a man whose name (whether Wister meant anything by it or not) is Balaam. A horse-torturer and killer, Balaam tries out Pedro and mistreats him; and the horse, not used to maltreatment, fights. Balaam kicks and beats him almost to death and finally gouges out one of Pedro's eyes. Between serial and novel publication, because of direct intervention from the President of the United States, his friend Theodore

Roosevelt, Wister toned the writing down to make it hard to tell exactly what Balaam did to Pedro. But the significant thing is what happens next:

> Then vengeance like a blast struck Balaam. The Virginian hurled him to the ground, lifted and hurled him again, lifted him and beat his face and struck his jaw. The man's strong ox-like fighting availed nothing. He fended his eyes as best he could against these sledge-hammer blows of justice. He felt blindly for his pistol. That arm was caught and wrenched backward, and crushed and doubled. He seemed to hear his own bones, and set up a hideous screaming of hate and pain. Then the pistol at last came out, and together with the hand that grasped it was instantly stamped into the dust. Once again the creature was lifted and slung so that he lay across Pedro's saddle a blurred, dingy, wet pulp.

Nowadays, of course, Wister's has become the classic horse-opera action of the cowboy in the white hat who never, no matter how rough the fight, loses the white hat or gets dirty, who is, in short, a superman. Wister's is the prototypical scene of neoromantic violence: a godlike hero meting justice with irresistible force, irresistible violence without reflex upon him, with no consequence for him. He is superhuman. Somewhere on television, at this moment, that fight is being re-enacted for the nth time; and watchers are learning one nth time more the fatally false lesson that violence does not really matter; that it has no real consequences because the good guy is invulnerable and the bad guy is "a creature." In the "effectist" world, violence is not real.

I I I

STEPHEN CRANE STARTED LIFE AS AN ATHLETE AND sports writer. When the secret of his almost instantaneous style is disclosed, some relationship to sports writing will appear, not only to Crane's own sports writing but to the kind of thing everybody was reading in the Nineties. In a famous letter Crane wrote to Lily Brandon on February 29, 1896, he says:

> You know, when I left you, I renounced the clever school in literature. It seemed to me that there must be something more in life than to sit and cudgel one's brains for clever and witty expedients. So I developed all alone a little creed of art which I thought was a good one. Later I discovered that my creed was identical with one of Howells and Garland and in this way I became involved in the beautiful war between those who say that art is man's substitute for nature and we are the most successful in art when we approach the nearest to nature and truth, and those who say—well, I don't know what they say. Than that they can't say much but they fight villainously and keep Garland and I out of the big magazines. Howells, of course, is too powerful for them.
>
> If I had kept to my clever Rudyard-Kipling style, the road might have been shorter but, ah, it wouldn't be the true road. The two years of fighting have been well-spent. And now I am almost at the end of it. This winter fixes me firmly. We have proved too formidable for them, confound them. They used to call me "that terrible, young radical," but now they are beginning to hem and haw and smile— those very old coons who used to adopt a condescending air toward me. There is an irony in the present situation that I enjoy, devil take them for a parcel of old, cringing, conventionalized hens.

Crane's irony directed against the neoromantics sounds wonderfully like Remington's irony directed against Howells.

It is easy to see violence deflated, sold out, in Crane: for instance, in a short story like "Horses—One Dash." This is the tale of Richardson, a New Yorker who finds himself in a Mexican inn taken over by *bandidos*. They are real bad men. At any moment they may break in, rob, and kill the *gringo*. After their carouse, however, the right moment comes. Richardson and his servant slip away, mount their horses, and off they dash to outrun the drunken *bandidos* and find safety. But at last the interesting thing is that, though Crane has toyed at length with the possibility of terrible violence, it never happened.

The same thing is true of "The Bride Comes to Yellow Sky," that ultimately reductive Western. The marshal decides that, after all, Yellow Sky has settled down, he can afford to get married. He gets on the train for San Anton, where he knows a waitress. They get married, and he brings her back. When he gets off the train, here is Scratchy Wilson, on a toot and shooting up Yellow Sky. The old conventions of Yellow Sky and its marshal and of being Scratchy Wilson, part-time Bad Man, demand that the marshal and Scratchy have a little shoot-out, after which the marshal will throw Scratchy in the calaboose to sober up. But the marshal has spoiled the game. In the first place he's married. Scratchy is bewildered and distraught. In the second place, the marshal is not armed. What can Scratchy do? Well, there isn't much for him to do. He puts his guns back in the holsters and slouches away into the sunset. Nothing has happened. The central myth of *The Police Gazette* has been undercut.

Still more explicit is "Five White Mice," which concerns one sober American kid in charge of two drunken friends in Mexico City. The drunks have insulted and mortally offended four knife-wielding citizens. The sober kid freezes his spine with a vision of their all being stabbed. Then he realizes that he might pull out his pistol and survive. With massive effort he musters the courage and draws. Of course the Mexicans pull back. Crane's last line is, "Nothing had happened."

IV

THE UNDERCUTTING OF VIOLENCE IN CRANE'S WEST-
ern tales relates to the applicability of the word "complicity" to "The Blue Hotel," as the far more complex and
subtle treatment of "The Open Boat" necessitates the
word "solidarity." Critics who wish to turn Crane into a
symbolist or perhaps a symbolic naturalist incline to conclude "The Blue Hotel" with its penultimate episode.
There the Swede, who has forcibly achieved death, lies
stabbed in the saloon with glazed eyes fixed on the cash-
register and its legend, "This registers the amount of
your purchase." But to stop there is to misrepresent
Crane's story. Crane wrote on through the final, intellectually climactic episode which draws the story and its
moral structure into focus. Here the Easterner and the
cowboy sit out on the prairie, discussing their experience.
The Easterner makes it plain that, though the gambler in
the saloon actually stabbed the Swede, it was not the
gambler who *murdered* him. The gambler served only as
a kind of incident or accident in a moral process. Guilt
belonged to the men personally concerned. They had
launched the Swede, maddened by conflict at the Blue
Hotel, upon the town and the innocent bystander of a
gambler in the saloon. The Easterner's gospel is Howells's doctrine of complicity: everyone shares in the guilt
of the world. Crane's injection of that doctrine into the
last scene of "The Blue Hotel" artfully reverses its moral
perspectives.

Against such backgrounds it is easier to understand
the violence in *Maggie: A Girl of the Streets*. The bar fight
in *Maggie* is wonderful. Perhaps there is not a better bar
fight in literature. Nevertheless, moral rather than
physical violence lies at the heart of the book. In the

Johnson household, to explain why Maggie went on the street, Crane stages a climactic fight. The mother, that ogre with the ironic name of Mary, having beaten her husband to death and spent most of her years since roaring drunk, has come to the point where Jimmie, her son, is able to beat her up and does:

> "Keep yer hands off me," roared his mother again. "Damn yer ol' hide," yelled Jimmie, madly. Maggie shrieked and ran into the other room. To her there came the sound of a storm of crashes and curses. There was a great final thump and Jimmie's voice cried: "Dere, damn yeh, stay still." Maggie opened the door now and went warily out. "Oh, Jimmie!"
>
> He was leaning against the wall and swearing. Blood stood upon bruises on his knotty fore-arms where they had scraped against the floor or the walls in the scuffle. The mother lay screeching on the floor, the tears running down her furrowed face.
>
> Maggie, standing in the middle of the room, gazed about her. The usual upheaval of tables and chairs had taken place. Crockery was strewn broadcast in fragments. The stove had been disturbed on its legs, and now leaned idiotically to one side. A pail had been upset and water spread in all directions.
>
> The door opened and Pete [the "elegant" bartender] appeared. He shrugged his shoulders. "Oh, Gawd," he observed.
>
> He walked over to Maggie and whispered in her ear. "Ah, what d' hell, Mag? Come ahn we'll have a hell of a time."
>
> The mother in the corner upreared her head and shook her tangled locks.
>
> "T' hell wid him and you," she said, glowering at her daughter in the gloom. Her eyes seemed to burn balefully. "Yeh've gone t' d' devil, Mag Johnson, yehs knows yehs have gone t' d' devil. Yer a disgrace t' yer people, damn yeh. An' now, git out an' go ahn wid dat doe-faced jude of yours. Go t' hell wid him, damn yeh, an' a good riddance. Go t' hell an' see how yeh likes it."

In a sense Maggie does what she must: go to hell. In another sense, by the time she goes to the river, what she has done is to vindicate the Mephistophelean observation from Marlowe, "Why this is hell, nor am I out of it," while she lives in her world. The whole book leads to the crushing irony of its last scene, when, Maggie dead, the neighbors come in and, with all the tearful sentimentality of the then equivalent of what is now soap opera, say to Mary, "You must forgive her." And she can't forgive: Maggie's a disgrace, she's ruined the family name—as if there were any family name—and the insufferably immoral daughter cannot be forgiven. But finally Mary screams, "Oh . . . I'll fergive her! I'll fergive her!"

Part of the point is, first of all, that in *Maggie* violence never exists independently, for its own sake; the other part is that the violence is (like the determinism) deeply, powerfully undercut.

The same things hold true for *The Red Badge of Courage*. Criticism too often forgets what the youth's "red badge of courage" actually was. His *red badge* served as Henry Fleming's forged passport back to his regiment after cowardly desertion under fire. It was a cut on the head taken from the rifle-butt of another deserter who was running so hard from the battlefield that when Henry tried to ask him what was happening the man simply clubbed him and dashed on.

There is no need to quote more from the text of the novel than one significant narrative aside which appears in its most violent section, Chapter 23. It comes when the regiment, after Fleming's return, has bungled assignments but acquired enough combat experience to know that it is regarded with contempt. The men are ordered to charge a fence-corner held by some Confederates and, somewhat to their own surprise, take it. They charge and discover that Confederates can run, too. Fleming, carrying the flag of his own outfit, captures the colors of the riddled Confederates. As they come away from what seemed like the conquest of an empire, the course of their heroic advance turns out to have been a couple of hundred yards of common meadow. And in the end their exploit has made no difference; they retreat.

As Fleming's regiment starts its charge,

> The youth kept the bright colors to the front. He was waving his free arm in furious circles, the while shrieking mad calls and appeals, urging on those that did not need to be urged, for it seemed that the mob of blue men hurling themselves on the dangerous group of rifles were again grown suddenly wild with an enthusiasm of unselfishness. [This kind of writing makes it credible that Crane learned about courage on the gridiron, not the battlefield.] From the many firings starting toward them, it looked as if they would merely succeed in making a great sprinkling of corpses on the grass between their former position and the fence. But they were in a frenzy, perhaps because of forgotten vanities. . . .

The short story called "The Veteran" reveals that the battle of *The Red Badge of Courage* was Chancellorsville, a series of inchoate fights which nobody won, though for the attacking Union Armies it was no victory. Stephen Crane's soldiers had a lesson to learn that is common to football, war, and human life: in spite of everything one might have done, in spite of sacrifice, wounds, and death, victory and defeat, courage and cowardice may have no final meaning. The universe regards the ego not. "The Veteran" deals with the eventual death of Henry Fleming. An old man, he dashes into the flames of a burning barn because screaming colts are trapped there. He does not need to inquire any longer whether he is courageous. He has already, in the same story, had the objectivity casually to tell local people that at Chancellorsville, his first battle, he had run. He goes into the flames because somebody ought to save the colts—because it's the right thing, in a sense the only thing, to do. The burning roof falls in on him, and the veteran is killed. The applicability of Crane's notion of "forgotten vanities" not only to the short story but to the novel is obvious.

V

THE REMARKABLE THING IS THE PARALLEL IN SENSE OF decorum between Howells and Crane. There is of course proportionately more violence in Crane. But both insist upon the same treatment of it, the same sense of limits, bounds, and restraint. They share the sense that violence must never stand alone as if it were an ultimate. They believe that a proper vision of reality cannot permit violence to stand without irony, without comic diminution.

Negatively, in other words, that shared vision functions as a kind of antiromanticism. The realism of Howells and Crane becomes a literature of respect, even reverence, for the comic. Negatively, it attacks superhumanism; it is anti-idealistic, anti-organicist, anti-egoistic. Positively, it stands upon a particular humanistic ground, the ground of a sensibility which is rational, compassionate, and reverential toward life.

Thus realism directs moral judgment against violence following a categorical imperative of decorum. One could lay the mere ideas out in a sort of heurism or paradigm. Realism opposed to neoromanticism suggests a sense of responsibility at war with commerciality—a problem much alive in our own time with its profound questions of what is happening to a population constantly exposed to the technologies of mass media enlisted in the service of a show-biz morality. Realism opposes compassion against the scientistic despair Robinson Jeffers called, elegantly, "inhumanism." Realism opposes a maturity of irony and self-irony against popular egotism and the indulgence of self.

Finally, it seems to me that some of the things Konrad Lorenz has had to say in *On Aggression* provide fresh perspective upon this topic. Central to Lorenz's concern is human self-betrayal, the dilemma of instinct betrayed by the mind while in the human condition our sole hope and dependence rest on the power of the mind to rescue itself from its own treachery. Lorenz holds out the crisis hope that man may be able to escape from the trap he has set for himself with mind-directed sublimations of aggression—like William James's "moral equivalent to war"—which are either symbolically violent, ritualistically limited, vicarious, or comic. Lorenz's ideas suggest that it was no mere way of handling literary, intellectual, or entertainment problems in the 1890's that the realists were getting at. They have something important to say to us about violence, about decorum, about reality now.

9 / The Virginian

W ITH ALL DUE RESPECT TO HIS LEARNED OPPONENTS ON THE subject, Henry James was right about *The Virginian*. It remains, as he said, "a rare and remarkable feat," notwithstanding its flaws and shortcomings. Patiently read, the style of James's letter of August 7, 1902 to Owen Wister in praise of the cowboy novel conveys precisely the Master's registration of the book's strengths and failures. Perhaps a too decided notion of James's fictional theories and tolerances has prevented both him and Wister from getting full credit for James's appreciation. The essence of what James wrote Wister follows:

> what I best like in it is . . . the personal & moral complexion & evolution, in short, of your hero . . . you have made him *live*. . . . & I find the whole thing a rare and remarkable feat. . . . nothing would have induced me to unite him to the little Vermont person, or to dedicate him in fact to achieved parentage, prosperity, maturity. . . . I thirst for his blood. I wouldn't have let him live & be happy; I should have made him perish in his flower & in some splendid sombre way.

I

JAMES IS RIGHT ABOUT THE ART OF THE VIRGINIAN'S character. As presented to us by the narrative persona of the dude, the cowboy in personality, action, attitude and, above all, talk is superb—as James says. He is a creation, endlessly interesting, and he *lives*. But James, however sympathetic to a friend, is also dead right about the main flaw in Wister's novel. He should have drowned the schoolmarm at the ford in her first scene. To develop her and her part in the novel, Wister had to switch from that sensitive register's point of view which brought him all his success to a smeary and naive omniscient-narrator's point of view. And most of that part of the novel dominated by naive omniscience became artistic wreckage. To get Molly Stark Wood and all she represents into his book, Wister had to sacrifice its esthetic integrities: and he paid the price. For reasons of obvious parallel, Wister's predicament recalls Fenimore Cooper and the unforgettable comment in James Russell Lowell's "A Fable for Critics." With all Cooper's shortcomings, says Lowell's Apollo,

> He has drawn you one character, though, that is new,
> One wildflower he's plucked that is wet with the dew
> Of this fresh Western world. . . . Natty Bumppo. . . .

> But . . . the women he draws from one model don't vary,
> All sappy as maples and flat as a prairie.

The truth about Wister's case, however, is not that the women of *The Virginian* are stereotyped. Frontier ruggedness, humanity, democracy and good sense are apparent in Mrs. Taylor. Wister was at least a mite daring in sketching the selective sensuality of the beautiful railroader's wife who kept an eating-house, repelled the traveling salesmen, and slept with the handsome cowboy. The trouble is not nearly so much that the schoolmarm is badly done on her own ground as that Wister chose the wrong ground for her. Howells had called attention the point in his 1895 review of *Red Men and White*. In spite of the authorial leanings toward melodrama, poesy, and "some guitar-tinkling," Howells said, the notable fact is the book's "intense masculinity"; it "is a man's book throughout." He admired Wister's humor, the skill with which he captured the veritable frontier, and especially the artfulness of his realism in presenting, uniquely well, a frontier politician, soldiers, and, above all else, Indians—"They convince of their truth: you feel that it is quite so they would think, and that their motives for good and ill would be almost for the first time in literature those attributed to them."

The right inference to draw from both James and Howells is that Wister could be extraordinarily good when he presented the West as he truly knew it. When he went wrong it was because he dealt in literary conventions or because he tried to reach for Significance—for the historical sense, the Meaning of the West.

As a whole, *The Virginian* simply cannot withstand critical analysis. There is no point in shattering cracked pots. The power of its masculinity and its wonderful matter give the book, and especially its hero, fine impetus and impact. But the lugged in significance exacts its price in bad art; Wister made a devil's bargain. Historically, his ill-wrought ideas were promptly displaced and forgotten. Popular and then mass-cult taste transformed his Great Western Novel into the Horse Opera of cinema and all its bastard progeny. If, as Upton Sinclair said, *The Jungle* was aimed at the heart of America but missed and hit its stomach, it might be said that Wister aimed at the historical imagination of America but struck the power-fantasy of modern man.

I I

NEVERTHELESS, IT IS INTERESTING TO SEE WHAT HAP-pened. What was Wister trying to say? What were those

ideas he tried to smuggle into his epic of Western chivalry behind the schoolmarm's skirts? The answers can be
found in certain relations of *The Virginian* to American
literary, intellectual, and cultural history. In those terms,
though Wister's intellectual aims were misguided, still
he was serious.

For parts of Wister's motivation it is useful to look to
his obvious American ancestor, Fenimore Cooper, and to
his friend and half-rejected mentor, Howells. Worldwide,
one of the archetypal themes of fiction has long been the
motif of Dick Whittington, or the Young Man from the
Provinces. Cooper, whose muse was Clio anyhow, saw
that the epic matter of the American frontier flowed in
a stream of the transit of culture from Europe down into
the wilderness and thence back up to civilization again.
He saw that the registry of movement (from wilderness to frontier to postfrontier to civilization in four
stages) and of cultural contrast were essential to an art
devoted to the matter of American history. He seems
to have known intuitively what all serious observers would confirm: that fraud and confusion followed
attempts to transport the frontier back East. To get at
the truth, one had to reverse the Whittington motif and
plunge civilized minds into the flowing process of the
West.

Characteristically, Cooper buried his clearest state-
ment of the theory of American historical dialectic that
informed all his best fiction except the sea novels. It appears as a narrative intrusion, explaining what had happened to "Templeton" (Cooperstown), in one of Cooper's
feebler fictions, *Home As Found*. The commentary is
worth quoting at some length because its observations
appear to have kept their validity for American imaginations as late as Hamlin Garland, Willa Cather, even Conrad Richter and Walter Van Tilburg Clark. The progress

of society, said Cooper, in "a 'new country,' is a little anomalous":

> At the commencement of a settlement, there is much of that sort of kind feeling and mutual interest which men are apt to manifest toward each other when they are embarked in an enterprise of common hazards. . . . Men, and even women, break bread together, and otherwise commingle, that, in different circumstances, would be strangers. . . . In this rude intercourse, the parties meet, as it might be, on a sort of neutral ground. . . . In short, the state of society is favorable to the claims of mere animal force, and unfavorable to those of the higher qualities.
>
> This period may be termed, perhaps, the happiest of the first century of a settlement. . . . Good-will abounds; neighbor comes cheerfully to the aid of neighbor; and life has much of the reckless gayety, careless association, and buoyant merriment of childhood. It is found that they who have passed through this probation usually look back to it with regret, and are fond of dwelling on the rude scenes and ridiculous events that distinguish the history of a new settlement, as the hunter is known to pine for the forest.
>
> To this period of fun, toil, neighborly feeling, and adventure, succeeds another, in which society begins to marshal itself, and the ordinary passions have sway.

Lacking as yet the awful intimation that the American doom was to be damnation by success, Cooper in his own middle phase distinguished his "epochs" as "pastoral," "equivocal," and "civilized." The Leatherstocking Tales he devoted to studying the transition from the wilderness period to the pastoral period. The Anti-Rent Trilogy, like *The Crater,* was given to a later Cooper's rage at intimations that perhaps his country could never make the final transit. But *Home As Found* confidently addressed to Cooper's countrymen his advice on how to make the best of their own advantages and of the resources of Europe, while avoiding the worst on both sides of the water, so as to triumph in fulfilling the destiny of the nation to create the best of all possible civilizations.

It would not, Cooper advised, be easy to make the transit. The "equivocal condition" is necessarily competitive, often mean and coarse, "perhaps the least inviting condition of society that belongs to any country that can claim to be free, and removed from barbarism." Like *Main-Travelled Roads, My Ántonia,* or *The Ox-Bow Incident,* Wister's novel deals with the matter of "the equivocal period." To make a long story short, *The Virginian* updates to the last frontier, on the fringe of industrialism, the whole of that theory of American history which Cooper developed for the Appalachian frontier on the fringe of agrarian civilization.

How much Wister's grasp of his intention coincided with Cooper's could be proved at once by paralleling the prefaces of *The Last of The Mohicans* and *The Deerslayer* with Wister's retrospective address "To the Reader" in *The Virginian.* Cooper and Wister both sought idealistically for an ultimate reality hidden behind the veiling actual; both appealed to the distancing perspectives of history as a means of seeing through the veil. Weir Mitchell's *Hugh Wynne,* and *The Scarlet Letter,* and *Uncle Tom's Cabin,* and *The Rise of Silas Lapham,* argued Wister, could all be said to be equally "historical." Why should he not share the privilege of snaring the past in art? He wrote:

> Had you left New York or San Francisco at ten o'clock this morning, by noon the day after to-morrow . . . you would stand at the heart of the world that is the subject of my picture, yet you would look around you in vain for the reality. It is a vanished world. No journeys, save those which memory can take, will bring you to it now. The mountains are there, far and shining, and the sunlight, and the infinite earth, and the air that seems forever the true fountain of youth,—but where is the buffalo, and the wild antelope, and where is the horseman with his pasturing thousands? So like

its old self does the sage-brush seem when revisited, that you wait for the horseman to appear.

But he will never come again. He rides in his historic yesterday. You will no more see him gallop out of the unchanging silence than you will see Columbus on the unchanging sea come sailing from Palos with his caravels. . . .

What is become of the horseman, the cow-puncher, the last romantic figure upon our soil? For he was romantic.

The chevalier of the wilderness plains was gone the way of the Leatherstocking, that natural knight of the big woods. If the Leatherstocking was, Cooper wrote in 1823, "the foremost in that band of Pioneers, who are opening the way for the march of the nation across the continent," the Virginian Wister perceived, with a pain not merely romantic, to be the last.

I I I

IT WAS ALL RIGHT, AS HOWELLS AND VALDÉS HAD agreed, to be honestly romantic. But suppose one were tempted merely to postulate ideal reality and then tell lies about the actual in support of his fraud? That would be "romanticistic." And suppose one were tempted to overcolor his vision and overorchestrate his technique to conceal mendacity? That would be "effectist."

No doubt because he was groping for the meaning of his extraordinary life's experience, a theme virtually obsessional with Howells was what he early explained to Henry James as the confrontation of a "conventional" with an "unconventional" person. That confrontation, progressively deepened in significance, was to be Howells's career-long method of Americanizing the motif of the Young Man (or Woman) from the Province. Though often enough in his large production the roles were reversed as to sex, what Howells was thinking of when he wrote to James was the ill-fated engagement of a man "conventionally" schooled in the graces, habits, assumptions, and snobberies of Society to a girl schooled in the "unconventions" of common, spontaneous, awkward, democratic American life. As Howells reversed Cooper's aristocratic values in favor of natural worth, genuineness and the common, in Wister those values threatened to become reversed again. Wister's heritage was glamorous and socially elevated. His treatment of the Virginian represented the sort of rebellion against established Society that Francis Parkman had mistakenly read into *The Rise of Silas Lapham*. Wister's own mother's resentment at what she saw as notions of ill-bred social climbing in *The Virginian* was at least as real as Parkman's.

In the end, however, the triumph of Wister's natural gentleman smacks more of Cooper than of Howells. On the whole, Wister shared Frederic Remington's sense of irritation toward his old friend and advisor of St. Botolph's Club; and part of the great difference from Howells was motivated by Social Darwinism. The new scientism looked back over the heads of the realists and their faith in the common. The presidency of Theodore Roosevelt, Howells said, turned American life back to the age before Andrew Jackson when "the gentle man" ruled the "common man." And Wister's view of the civilizing process could have been expressed in Cooper's words: "Civilization" means "the division into castes that are more or less rigidly maintained, according to circumstances." It was over some such notion that Molly Stark Wood and her Vermont D. A. R. kinfolk agonized when they feared she had fallen in love with a frontier vulgarian.

The most interesting minor figure sketched in *The Virginian* is Shorty, the pitiful anticowboy from Brooklyn. Shorty is, at everything except affection for Pedro his horse, an incompetent. And Wister sees it to be the law of the West, the law of nature obeyed by man under the awful thumb of nature, that incompetence must die. Even worse, the doom of incompetence is contagious; strong men foolishly allied with it die too. The strong, and intelligence and integrity are strengths as much as hard muscles or fine coordination, live and win. The weak go down. Victorious, successful, the fittest, the Virginian was Shorty's polar opposite, nature's Darwinian gentleman of the West, and therefore worthy.

Though nobody seems to have studied the question adequately, there can be little doubt that the neoromantics, acting out Social Darwinism in life and art, helped to change American sexual mores around the turn of the century. Explicit in *The Virginian* is the notion of a real, essential masculine principle in the West and the cowboy confronting a sleepy feminine principle in Molly Stark Wood. In the Virginian himself a wild masculine principle, too easily isolated and antisocial, needs to be cultivated and made responsible: it must be civilized. But Molly needs to crack the shell of dead puritanism around her Vermont femininity. She must break out and leave behind the effete Easternism of a sexual genteel tradition. Within herself the feminine principle must be recognized, refreshed, and invigorated. To accept her cowboy lover is to confront and accept her own sexuality primitivized and set free. Conceivably because Wister did not dare, but more likely because he did not know how to treat of a lady in the same universe of sexual discourse with the mistress of the boarding house, he fell into an effectism for which there is a good old word, "mawkish."

The anticlimax which is the best Wister can bring to the eventual honeymoon in the Rockies really says everything:

They made their camps in many places, delaying several days here, and one night there, exploring the high solitudes together, and sinking deep in their romance. Sometimes when he was at work with their horses, or intent on casting his brown hackle for a fish, she would watch him .with eyes that were fuller of love than of understanding. Perhaps she never came wholly to understand him; but in her complete love for him she found enough. He loved her with his whole man's power. She had listened to him tell her in words of transport, 'I could enjoy dying'; yet she loved him more than that. He had come to her from a smoking pistol, able to bid her farewell—and she could not let him go. At the last white-hot edge of ordeal, it was she who renounced, and he who had his way. Nevertheless she found much more than enough, in spite of the sigh that now and again breathed through her happiness when she would watch him with eyes fuller of love than of understanding.

There was, finally, an esthetic Nemesis which pursued the faithlessness of the neoromantics.

And from the other "climax" of *The Virginian* one can see that an avenging justice camped on the trail of "the romanticistic" as well as "effectism." Wister was evidently self-compelled to bind all the other elements of his book with the sexual into one well-wrapped package of respectability. To avoid that, James told him, the master novelist would have let the Virginian "perish in his flower & in some splendid sombre way." As the novel stands, it supposes that all's well that ends well; and the cowboy ends as an entrepreneur. His success represents a standard neoromantic worship of the bitch-goddess on a Social Darwinian altar. In the perspectives of American cultural history, Wister ended by aligning his creation with the extractive-exploitative tradition of the Western rape of nature which, cubed, has brought us to the crisis of a technological culture on the edge of drowning in its own excreta. Wister's neo-Hamiltonian, Whiggish, "American Way" romanticization of the business mind was much like Cooper's, too, except that Wister substituted the tycoon for the Squire.

In the wake of Trampas and his ilk, the cattle war came in 1892,

> ... when, after putting their men in office, and coming to own some of the newspapers, the thieves brought ruin on themselves as well. For in a broken country there is nothing left to steal.
>
> But the railroad came, and built a branch to that land of the Virginian's where the coal was. By that time he was an important man, with a strong grip on many various enterprises, and able to give his wife all and more than she asked or desired. Sometimes she missed the Bear Creek days, when she and he had ridden together, and sometimes she declared that his work would kill him. But it does not seem to have done so. Their eldest boy rides the horse Monte; and, strictly between ourselves, I think his father is going to live a long while.

Serious models of civilization failed Wister as they failed Cooper. But the doomed knight of the wilderness succeeds with the reader because he first succeeded with the imagination of the author. The Leatherstocking and the Virginian live on in their books. Is it their fault, or their authors', or ours that, essentialized to pure vulgarity, they have provided a grist, endlessly regrindable like the dust of the moon, for the mills of the entertainment industry?

10 / Teacher's Choice

I T IS IMPOSSIBLE TO DENY THAT HISTORICALLY THE NOVEL IN America has suffered a diminution. Of late years, news about its demise has been featured in middlebrow journals almost as regularly as seasonal announcements of the death of the theater. Though the corpse is far too lively for burial, it would be impossible to adopt for our time the bold words of Frank Norris at the turn of the century: "Today is the day of the novel . . . and by no other vehicle is contemporaneous life as adequately expressed." Because it spoke vitally to "the People," the American novel had become, Norris said, "the great bow of Ulysses," its influence "greater than all the pulpits, than all the newspapers between the oceans." The responsibilities of the novelist Norris thought therefore morally ultimate.

With a vastly greater potential market, even "best-sellers" rarely do better today than their equivalents in Norris's time: and what contemporary novel can boast anything like the national impact of *The Jungle* or *Babbitt* or *The Grapes of Wrath* when they were new? Obviously there has occurred a decline which is partly a function of that experimentation with forms and that alienation in the artist which have issued in the "antinovel." Partly, also, the diminished impact of the novel is a function of shifts, basically technological, in the entertainment industries. Television and "do it yourself" in the home and family circle, and radio in the car, with the once omnipotent movies a fading fourth, have crowded the novel out of popular preeminence.

Nevertheless, insofar as "the People" read, and for a literate class far greater in absolute numbers than before, the novel still leads the field. Its decline is relative to mass-cult phenomena. Relative to other literary forms it remains the Queen. And there remain reasons for taking it seriously, reasons of the utmost cogency for teachers of American literature.

We have a fairly general agreement concerning the function of fiction. If in mass terms the teacher's problem with the novel is a Frostian one of knowing what to do with a diminished thing, esthetically there is no dilemma. A successful novel is a successful work of art. As such, it may order and intensify our inward, most significant experience and satisfy our thirst for that irreducible event we call beauty. It succeeds esthetically on the same terms as other art; and the problems of "teaching" it are the same as with other modes of literature: we must discover and know how to employ enticements and incitements which will lead our students to experience for themselves something of what is potentially there for them.

But there are ways in which long prose fiction is different, too. It *is* prosy and discursive. It has room for mass and breadth and lengths of time—time of many sorts within and without its webs of illusion. It can afford the luxuries of multiple points of view: the author's, narrator's, reader's, and of course those of characters. It can look and listen closely, or at any middle distance, or in the grandest panoramas of space and history. It can stage scenes, paint pictures, present with utter impartiality— or summarize, foreshorten, interpret, imagine, symbolize: do anything its author's virtuosity can dream of. Seldom matching the intensity of poetry or the immediacy of theater, the novel has freedoms and immunities (so far as one can really differentiate the genres, of course) not granted its rivals.

I

THE NOVEL THEREFORE IS POTENTIALLY SUPREME AS A mode of social—and thus in our case of American—definition. There are many good reasons to study and teach it well. Since that is true; and since the study of American literature has always had as one of its chief motives the derivation of main images of American definition from the possibilities suggested by literary works; and since we have been in the presence of an unprecedented "explosion of knowledge" in the field—no minor part of which has been devoted to the novel—it might legitimately be expected that among studies of fiction there should have appeared a work of literary and national definition of major distinction, some monument of original interpretation and synthesis. Although there have been a number of excellent and important studies of American novelists and their work, unfortunately that greatly to be wished for masterwork seems not to exist. Has there been a study of the American novel comparable in force of general illumination, for instance, to F. J. Hoffman's *The Twenties,* Lewis's *The American Adam,* Spencer's *The Quest for Nationality,* or Pearce's *The Continuity of American Poetry?* I think not.

Many readers will at once detect the absence from the foregoing list of an ambitious and famous account of

American fiction: *The American Novel and Its Tradition* by the late Richard Chase. It has dominated many college classrooms for a decade or more and raised up schools of criticism in a tradition of its own. Obviously I am committed to some effort to explain why I do not think it sufficiently a success to be classed with the superior works I have named as standards of comparison.

If there is in our times no need to respect the superstition of *de mortuis nil nisi bonum,* still, and especially in the recent absence of a potent mind, there may seem to be something less than sporting in passing judgment on his work. He cannot defend himself. My generation of "American literature men" suffered tragic decimation in the deaths of four scholars. Richard Chase, Charles Fenton, Frederick J. Hoffman, and Stephen Whicher were fine minds near the height of their powers when they died. We cannot spare any of them; but one of the liveliest and furthest-ranging was Chase. My excuses for criticizing his work are that he would never have wished anyone's judgment inhibited by other than intellectual considerations and that toward the end he himself was moving away from some of the commitments of his book and toward certain of the notions I shall urge against them.

It is not easy to feel that one does justice to a literary mind so acute, so well-stocked, so concerned, so passionate as Chase's by any sort of cavil. But the word which recurs to me as I consider what I find lacking in his book is "responsibility." Obviously one cannot feel that the passionate moral, cultural, and professional concerns evident in his work suggest "irresponsibility" in any common sense. How could one care more than he? Therefore "responsibility" must have particular implications in the present context, and it is my duty to try to make those implications clear.

We might all agree concerning *The American Novel*

and Its Tradition that it is in many respects a brilliant work to which a tradition of subsequent books stands in debt. It might have become that masterwork for which we look, and to consider it a candidate for that distinction is high praise. The necessary question becomes, What is wrong or lacking? *Why* is Chase's work not finally satisfactory? Let us begin to answer by admitting that of course there never was a book in which the carping mind could find no flaw, exactly as there is no construction of the human mind which can triumph over a determined scepticism. As the latter is the point of David Hume, the former is the point of the ancient exclamation: "O that mine enemy would write a book!"

Since the author is no enemy, however, one has to acknowledge the candle-power of his illuminating central thesis, the penetration of his sharp insights into the qualities of ideas as well as fictional esthetics. It is a good, important book. But it is not always bright or sharp. It suffers from weaknesses in structural coherence and in the regular, progressive, and cumulative development of themes. Like many another book it promises introductorily to develop and demonstrate by analyses of individual authors and novels claims for the validity of its thesis which are in fact not proved, or which perhaps have become seriously qualified by the time the analyses actually appear. But these are normal limitations and failings of the nodding human mind, to be forgiven in admiration for the achievements of a book. Less forgivable in Chase are lapses in intellectual method, especially the tendency to free and easy word-juggling and sleight-of-hand transformations with such terms as "myth," "archetype," "exorcism," "Calvinism," "real," "reality," "realism," "melodrama," even "romance" and "novel." Still harder to accept are the gaps, the absences of essential writers, books, and aspects of books which are simply not present to the total *oeuvre* of the American novel presented in Chase's volume.

It is Chase's thesis that the "best" and most characteristically American fiction is "romance" distinguished for "rapidity, irony, abstraction, profundity . . . a brilliant and original, if often unstable and fragmentary, kind of literature," a literature of "romantic nihilism, a poetry of force and darkness." This is a fiction which he says "proceeds from an imagination that is essentially melodramatic," which "tends to carve out of experience brilliant, highly wrought fragments rather than massive unities." That imagination, Chase reiterates, has been made profound but "narrow and Manichean" by American circumstances. It can have no vital apprehension of social reality but must be violent, radical, symbolistic, poetic, archetypal, metaphysical, alienated, terrible, and discontinuous if not chaotic. In this list one finds virtually all the "OK words" of what was once revered as "modern criticism." By their acute application, Chase is able to treat as critically respectable a considerable body of more or less "standard" American fiction. But it is revealing to notice the price exacted for his ability to do this. One is tempted to conclude that it might have been better to sacrifice "modernity" and keep American literature.

To make the briefest list, Chase's account of American fiction reveals the following deficiencies. He overemphasizes the importance and misemphasizes for tactical purposes the nature of the fiction of Charles Brockden Brown. If one were looking candidly for "archetypes" of the American novel it would be impossible to overlook Brackenridge's *Modern Chivalry* with its essential anticipations of Cooper, Hawthorne, Melville, Howells, James, Twain, Hemingway, Faulkner, and Bellow, to name the obvious. In general one would suppose from

Chase that there had been no picaresque tradition in American fiction. The central historical and therefore tragic vision of Cooper is ignored. Chase allies himself with the Jamesian heresy in denying intellectual and moral seriousness to Hawthorne: among other things that permits him to remark that Hester Prynne "becomes a kind of social worker." Chase may be right in holding *Billy Budd* not to be a work of Christian vision; but it seems hardly adequate to conclude hastily that it is "conservative" in the mode of Edmund Burke.

The second half of Chase's book, treating of American fiction since Melville, seems less satisfactory than the first. Though that was intellectually perhaps the fatefulest half-century of our history, Chase seems to recognize no developments in American thought between, say, 1845 and 1895; and the urbanization and industrialization of our culture would appear not to have occurred. Though his long discussion of *The Portrait of a Lady* finally becomes sound, the chapter begins, for evident purposes of connection with the thesis, on a note of misemphasis which implies a false conclusion and from which the discussion recovers with difficulty. Even then, though the tragic irony of what is at length admitted to be a novel, not a romance, is at last acknowledged, Chase misses one of the most mordant effects of the book, its critical irony, its perspective of "negative realism" in which the immoralities of Isabel Archer's romantic egotism are exposed and punished. Little is said of the rest of James. One could go on with such a list; but, though I am tempted to complain of the maltreatment of Howells, the misdirections of the curt section on Twain, and the disregard of Stephen Crane and Dreiser, I trust my point is made.

Chase's thesis that the Americanness of our fiction consists in romance, not novel, is nevertheless argued persuasively. At its best in his hands the thesis becomes an excellent critical instrument—as far as it goes. Taken instrumentally and partially, it becomes a ground for useful insights. Taken exclusively, however, as a unitary generalization which proposes that essential American qualities and expression are only romantic, it becomes not just needlessly limiting but demonstrably false. A good test is to see that one might write another study to show that fundamental American qualities and expression have been and are also novelistic—that is, social, rational, apollonian, common, realistic, and ironic. That would perhaps be equally enlightening. It would also, given the recent state of critical fashion, be at least equally original.

Behind his exclusive claim for "the romance" there had to lie an assumption of which the history of literary criticism ought to have made Chase wary. Because recent criticism lauded "romance" values and modernist criticism frequently succumbed to the temptation to conflate literary values with cultural and so with cultural-historical theories, Chase was led to argue that "Manichean melodramatic" romances were the best and most characteristic features of what he loosely called "the American imagination." The dubiousness of some of his intellectual procedures not considered, the histories of taste and criticism should have reminded Chase that it is naive to suppose that any one set of literary judgments will endure. The puzzled clergyman in Robert Frost's "The Black Cottage" said, "Most of the change we think we see in life/ Is due to truths being in and out of favour." It was perhaps an irritating thing to say; but he was wise.

Surely one would do well to suspect in the present what we have learned to look for in the past. There we have learned to seek behind the styles of mind the bases of fashion in judgment and ask in particular how viable were the unspoken, then unspeakable, assumptions upon which judgment was grounded. Such learning inclines one toward pluralism and the intellectual principles of uncertainty and indeterminacy. But the situation presented in Chase's book gives to wonder how sufficiently aware he was, when he wrote the book, of his own grounds. After the book had been in print a while, he underwent the normal experience of a sensitive author and began to feel suspicious of those grounds. Doubts and afterthoughts were evident in Chase's review article on Leslie Fiedler's *Love and Death in the American Novel* in 1960. Chase thought Fiedler awkwardly imitative and a bit obsolescent. The article is tendentious, paradoxical, often sassy, and finally important. It reminds us again how sore a loss we suffered in the author's death, for it shows Chase in transit from his earlier critical self toward what I choose to think would have been a more valuable maturity. As I understand him, Chase was there urging us to look beyond the apocalyptic mood and method toward more pluralistic, historical, realistic, and syncretistic ways.

I I

REVIEWING FIEDLER, CHASE SEEMS BASICALLY TO have been suggesting a new view of himself as "postmodern." And in so doing he had begun to align himself in relationship to phenomena which teachers of American literature have so far only dimly grasped. To put it flatly, the "modernist" period in our culture is historical. A crucial difference between "modernism" and the contemporary is that nowadays almost nobody can feel proud to be "up to date."

If there were many proud American "modernisms" between the Massachusetts Bay experiment and Walt

Whitman's ringing, portentous "Years of the Modern," when twentieth-century modernism took shape it was in a mood far less confident, heroic, or nationalistic. There had intervened a complex, ambiguously happy and disastrous time during which a rustic, provincial people were transformed into a mighty but incomplete industrial nation and thrust upon the stage of world significance. During the same period, the disintegrative forces of an incredible century fell upon American culture: industrialization, urbanization, a population explosion intensified by millions of immigrants, social and economic problems of a scale, a newness, and a suddenness without precedent; in a representative democracy, political problems to match; after 1898, involvement in the grand imperial game of the powers; eventually, participation in global wars.

Together with overt revolutions came reverberating crises in thought, the ground of culture. There were first the terrible challenges to anthropology and teleology—and hence to religious tradition and practice—which fame clusters about the name of Darwin. Then the challenges to social institutions, political patterns, and economic practices which cluster about the name of Marx. Then the challenges to the integrity of the personality, to the respectability, perhaps even the existence, of the self that are associated with Freud. And lastly the challenges to the factuality, the human availability, perhaps even to the actuality of nature which attach to the name of Einstein.

Much of the first thirty years of this grand change was summed up in such works as Howells's *A Hazard of New Fortunes;* Stephen Crane's poetry; Mark Twain's "Mysterious Stranger" manuscripts; and *The Education of Henry Adams.* But after World War I the feeling of deracination of the young American artist intensified to the point where he tended to repudiate with blind indignation every manifestation of "The Old Gang." As the best student of the "moderns," Frederick J. Hoffman, put it, they were fired by a "useful innocence." Innocence lent them courage and energy while it concealed their confusions. It carried them into what Joseph Wood Krutch, in a famous book, called *The Modern Temper.*

To follow Hoffman in his superb analysis entitled *The Twenties,* that temper of which the "modernists" were so conscious in themselves was innocently blended of contradictions. The most basic was the paradox of a confidence in the superior wisdom, sanity, honesty, and humanity of the present (the "New Gang" over the "Old Gang")—a confidence as sweeping as Whitman's—combined with bitter disillusion, a despair overwhelmingly adolescent in mood. Surveying the age from its center in 1931, the wise and elegant philosopher Irwin Edman commented:

> The whole of the modern temper has been a fretful canvassing of the conditions of the soul of man under mechanism, industry and latter-day worldliness. . . . one begins by doubting the existence of the soul; one ends by doubting whether its interests can be fulfilled, or whether in the long run they matter. . . . The whole attempt of contemporary reflection may be said to be that of finding some way of life whereby the modern may find integrity or peace. . . . Little, one is tempted to say, has more crucified the contemporary meditating upon himself than this sense of irremediable evil, of something beyond salvage and not deserving it.

The lines of modernist force converged to produce a furious critical attack against contemporaneous American culture, an attack expressed largely in shibboleths. Traditional supernaturalism and religious practice, conventional morality (especially restraints upon sexuality), and the contradictions between formal Christianity and common social or economic morality were assailed as "Puritanism." Popular bourgeois taste and the Franklin tradition of use before beauty were scorned as "Philistinism." In a famous portmanteau pun, Mencken excoriated the entire middle-class ethos as characteristic of "the booboisie." Sinclair Lewis's hero provided a fleering term for the aims and values of the business mind and its practitioners—"Babbittry"; "a Babbitt." At the same time, every effort to domesticate the heritages of the past in American life fell under the condemnation of George Santayana's contemptuous phrase, "the genteel tradition."

As the modernist decades passed, however, it became apparent that the energy of the movement had been culturally more destructive than creative. It produced a great critical art. What the thunder said in T. S. Eliot's "The Wasteland" rumbled far away. Lewis's wonderful satire raveled out into vague inanities. When the carnival of denials was over, not much was left to live for or by. Freedom had been gained from very much, but it appeared decreasingly clear what freedom had been gained for. To the modernist there often seemed left only a religion of art, and that was sometimes snatched away by impulses such as that of Dada. Even the art-religion became linked to an experimentalism that threatened to put an end to communication—as for most readers of *Finnegans Wake* or Ezra Pound's *Cantos* it did.

Despite what seemed to the modern temper its sharp sophistication and dark wisdom, in other words, it appears in retrospect to have been naive, innocent, and provincial—and to have based itself largely on an unacknowledged cultural confidence impossible to sustain. If O'Neill and Eliot, Frost, and Faulkner, and Hemingway continue to stand out of that time, it may be because they came to have something more to offer: not innocence but, beyond innocence, responsibility.

The end of the "modern" period was early noted by Randall Jarrell and ratified by Stephen Spender. But, especially in the light of *The Modern Temper,* even more interesting and authoritative was the article, "Challenge to an Unknown Writer," by Joseph Wood Krutch. Thirty-three years—technically an exact historical generation—after the publication of his epoch-making book, Krutch announced himself prepared for another age. He summarized brilliantly the iconoclasm, disassociationism, and libertarianism of the earlier period while observing sadly that these seem to have delivered their devotees into ennui and confusion. Intellectuals, he complained, are split into two noncommunicating groups: the "social engineer" doers who seek a material Utopia through manipulative techniques; the thinkers, "verging toward . . . nihilistic despair," who "recommend only that we strive toward that existential resignation which makes the absurd acceptable." He acknowledged the danger that "we seem to be headed for a civilization in which everybody will be content except the thinkers—who have grown desperate."

Having disposed of the iconoclastic innocence which hoped that if enough "half gods" were smashed the gods would arrive, Krutch proceeded to deny the mechanistic theory that literature can only reflect its age. He called upon the writer to play his part in creating his age—a new one. And he ended by pointing out that only five years after writing *The Modern Temper* he himself had "ceased to believe that getting rid of half gods was sufficient" and had said:

> If Love and Honor and Duty can be salvaged, then someone must write about them in a fashion which carries

conviction. If we are to get along without them, then some-
one must describe a world from which they are absent in
a fashion which makes that world seem worth having. And
it is just the failure to do either of these things quite adequately which reveals the weakness of contemporary literature.

Krutch's charge to the "unknown writer" is, of
course, the converse of what he thinks the "weakness of
contemporary literature." However, it has seemed to me
for some time that it was that motion of the greatest
contemporary American writers to anticipate Krutch's
call as long ago as the 1940's which marked the beginning
of the end of modernism. Frost had always stood out, long
to the damage of his reputation. Eliot had turned mag-
nificently in his wartime poetry, *Four Quartets,* and his
postwar plays. Hemingway had done the same in *For
Whom the Bell Tolls* and *The Old Man and the Sea.*
Faulkner in his Nobel Prize speech made explicit what
one had sensed in his work and what he emphasized in
the careful resetting of his hunting stories entitled *Big
Woods,* 1955.

Post modern poets like W. D. Snodgrass, the late
Theodore Roethke, and Robert Lowell may be emerging
as responsibilitists in accord with Faulkner's or Krutch's
call. Even more striking, however, has been the case of a
major novelist who perhaps falls between the epochs.
Robert Penn Warren was born in 1905; his first novel was
not published until 1939 and his first significant one not
until 1946. The dating of literary "periods" is always a
shaky business. One student of twentieth-century American literature whose judgment I respect says that 1938
marks the end of the "modern" period. Others might say
1940, with the attacks of Van Wyck Brooks, Archibald
MacLeish, and Bernard DeVoto on "the irresponsibles,"
and "the literary fallacy." It is entirely possible that the

historian of the future will wish to say that its end was marked by the publication of *All The King's Men*, 1946, the first "postmodern" novel.

The distinguishing mark of Warren's kind of fiction may well lie in the sense of life expressed in the last sentence of *All The King's Men*. With the long agony and catastrophe of the book's tragedy done, the hero-narrator concludes, "soon now we shall go out of the house and go into the convulsions of the world, out of history into history and the awful responsibility of Time." Warren's men are voyagers on a stream of time which bears reality and value in its continuity. Experience taught Jack Burden "how if you could not accept the past and its burden there was no future, for without one there cannot be the other, and how if you could accept the past you might hope for the future, for only out of the past can you make the future."

For Warren time becomes real as history. And he has powerfully revivified the historical novel as a form in which to express his vision of that process. To do so required a major effort of the esthetic imagination. When serious fiction came of age artistically in the late nineteenth century, the historical novel was relegated, as by Howells and James, to the realm of the nonserious. Their objection was psychological: historical characterizations must always be anachronistic; the writer can truly know only the psychic colorations of his own time and place and must falsely paint the people of the past with his own psychic pigments.

No matter how vastly popular, historical fiction was thus exiled from the serious center to the irresponsible periphery of art. It was only romance. And even as, in our time, the wheel has revolved, realism gone down and romanticism up with the ascendancy of "mythic" modes of apprehension, historical fiction has largely remained romance. Warren's problem was to retain the serious novel's engagement with real persons in real time, with the palpable textures of social force and moral concern, but still be free to deal with time actualized in experience, with history.

His solution has been brilliant. To take our one example, *All the King's Men* treats of a case obviously like that of Governor Huey Long of Louisiana. If Warren is deeply concerned to fix the texture and meaning of contemporary events, he is still more concerned to place events in the whole context of social, psychic, and moral development in the American South. To present perspectives, he invents as hero and sensitive consciousness, or "register," and narrator of his tale a disillusioned intellectual, scion of the old elite, a newspaper man and trained historical scholar. Jack Burden can participate both directly and vicariously at every significant contemporary level of the action. But because he has a trained historical imagination; because he and Warren know that history is not so much a matter of scientific investigation as it is a special art of knowing how to imagine the significance of data; and because Warren ingeniously creates a set of historical documents upon which the reader can watch Burden's historical imagination at work, the final effect is convincing. We do indeed see men and women go "out of history into history and the awful burden of Time."

In other Warren novels there are sometimes even more admirable presentations of his vision. But it must suffice here to say that for Warren the awful burden of time is the post-Edenic weight of man's accepted guilt, his accepted need for moral action, his responsibility. There may be, it is not easy to tell, a post-Kierkegaardian sort of Christianity in this view, demythologized as Bultmann or Tillich would wish it and remythologized in the esthetic imagination of the novelist. Or there may be simply still another kind of humanism.

For myself I should wish to say that work like Warren's gives one faith in the possibilities of the period of which one can only so far say that it is "contemporary" or "postmodern." The very fact of his cult of disillusion testified to the real innocence and security of the modernist. He could afford the sentimental luxuries of gloom. Now we have, with clear eyes and hearts chastened by historical reality, to create a life for man which can survive, and deserves morally to survive, in a world where what used to be chimeras have become horrifyingly real. Warren has been expert at showing us such horrors—and then to show that we can afford the luxuries neither of horror nor of hysteria. Warren's sort of responsibility means the acceptance, not the suicidal rejection, of man's moral and spiritual guilt, his complicit involvement in the histories of his race, his culture, his nation.

I I I

IN THESE PERSPECTIVES THE QUESTION BECOMES NOT merely whether by ignoring and misemphasizing things Chase and his school do not mistake the American novel but whether they do not actually falsify it. Much of the blame for the deficiencies in Chase's work can be laid at the door of the critical attitude called "apocalyptic." It is noteworthy that D. H. Lawrence's *Studies in Classic American Literature* have constituted a sort of scripture for Chase and his followers. But I think their discipleship to Lawrence more symptomatic than causal. The "apocalyptic" attitude is analogous to the existentialist despair in philosophy or the "crisis-theology" of our times. They are symptoms of cultural crisis.

What is for me a helpful light is cast on the situation

by Professor Armin Arnold's study of the emergent compositional stages of Lawrence's famous book. Of three successive "versions" of Lawrence's text, the first two expressed his sense of the American dream. They were "written in a very moderate, explanatory tone . . . logical, intelligent, and well-observed," says Arnold, and the ideas were neatly supported by quotation. But the third, the version published, was "hysterical." It was written at a peak of "violent hatred," Arnold explains, with Lawrence, "in a state of extreme nervous tension resulting in almost insane outbreaks against his wife, his friends, his animals, against America as a whole." The author's rage was reflected in the "exaggerated, shrieking style of the book."

It always sounded as if something hysterical, certainly nothing responsible in the ordinary meaning of the word, found expression in *Studies in Classic American Authors*. Why then take it as a form of scripture? Because, I think the answer has to be, one feels outraged —and thus outrageous—as Professor Fiedler felt in reviewing Professor Walter Blair's *Mark Twain and Huck Finn* for the *New York Times Book Review* of April 3, 1960. The review complains that Blair is "reasonable" rather than "adventurous," "outrageous," or "witty and terrible." It blames Blair for avoiding "risky speculation in favor of safe facts" and for not confronting "the deeper questions" such as the "fact" that Twain knew that his book "projected *symbolically* an order of truth unavailable to history or sociology." And it concludes:

> It is well to remember that the first 'psychological critic' of Huck Finn was . . . a nineteenth-century printer who, making an obscene addition to one of 'Huck's' illustrations . . . commented on a weakness in its view of life that even Twain's humor and the sweet reasonableness of scholars cannot finally conceal.

"Sweet" or not, reasonableness demands a comment on Fiedler's notion of criticism. As Blair had informed the reviewer (and most other people), some one in the print-shop who did not love his employer turned one of E. W. Kemble's illustrations into a sly, dirty joke. On page 283 of the first edition of *Adventures of Huckleberry Finn* the picture shows Uncle Silas, bent slightly backward and with open mouth. At his left is Aunt Sally wearing a fond, foolish grin; and facing Silas, with head at the man's vest-pocket level, is Huck. The cut-line says, "Who do you reckon it is?" In plates just suppressed in time to save the author, the firm, and the book from public disgrace, some jokester had drawn something like an exposed and erect penis on Uncle Silas.

Inspection of one of the rare altered plates is a visually dull experience. It was a feeble joke, and for purposes of literary criticism the plates deserve to be rare. The joke was not Huck's or Twain's; it was not even Kemble's. A wry sidelight on publishing history, the suppressed plate simply has nothing to do with *Adventures of Huckleberry Finn* as a book or as literature. And the prankster was "the first 'psychological critic'"?

Something of a like antipathy to "sweet reasonableness" appears to have motivated Chase's love for the wild symbolisms of Manichean melodrama and to have tempted him occasionally to leap toward an arbitrary and far-fetched bit of free association in the guise of criticism. Such is his doubly misplaced observation that, in Cooper's *The Prairie*, Natty Bumppo "sadly watches" the Bush family "with exactly the same feelings aroused in Faulkner's Ike McCaslin by people like the Snopes family." Or the dictum that *The Scarlet Letter*

. . . incorporates its own comic-book or folklore version. Chillingworth is the diabolical intellectual, or perhaps even the mad scientist. Dimmesdale is the shining hero or to more sophisticated minds the effete New Englander. Hester is the scarlet woman, a radical and nonconformist, partly 'Jewish' perhaps (there is at any rate an Old Testament quality about her. . . . Like many other American writers, Hawthorne is not entirely above the racial folklore of the Anglo-Saxon peoples. . . . as in Hawthorne's *Marble Faun,* Miriam is Jewish, in Melville's *Pierre* Isabel is French, and in *Billy Budd* Claggart is dimly Mediterranean). Pearl is sometimes reminiscent of Little Red Riding Hood or a forest sprite of some sort who talks with the animals. Later when she inherits a fortune and marries a foreign nobleman, she is the archetypal American girl of the international scene, like the heroines of Howells and James.

In short, anybody may say anything about literature that pops into his head. If Chase's fantasy was not merely incoherent, it was certainly not responsible to the sort of reasonableness Walter Blair and I agree in thinking essential to ordinary intellectual communication. It was, I should urge, not at all "responsible" but merely personal and arbitrary, a form of self-indulgent self-expression. Why, then, to ask the question in another way, should a Richard Chase, clearly an expert practitioner of reasonable discourse, have chosen to throw responsibility away?

He seems to have been attracted to the "apocalyptic" method by a sense of the intellectual history everybody knows. When they were not somehow merely traditionally Christian, the Old-American attitudes toward life and literature before, say 1870, were either rationalistically and commonsensically moral or idealistically romantic. After 1870 they tended to change toward acceptance of an agnostic but still public if, as Howells put it, "unmoralized" morality. But with the growing triumph by the end of the century of a thoroughly reductive, "naturalistic" sensibility reinforced in our century both by a terrible history and by the theories of man suggested in Pavlov and Freud, there ensued almost total revolt. It became a favorite American way to express this as revolt against "unreality" and "the genteel tradition." Cumulatively the revolt threatened to do away with the "gentilities" of moralism, whether avowed or implied; then with ideality of faith or concept; then with personalism; and finally with mere order. One way to escape from the personal crises which made a part of the cultural crisis thus discovered was for those convulsed to turn to desperate faith.

And perhaps the "crisis-faith" most readily available has been faith in naked, violent assertion of the self, whether that self could be supposed warranted by "reality" or not. Hence a neo-neoromanticism of "apocalypse" and, critically, a revaluation of American fiction in apocalyptic terms. Hence the acceptability of Laurentian outrage. I suppose, in short, the ground of the attitude shared by Chase and Fiedler to be a conviction that our culture is dead or dying and one's expressive duty is to register his desperate sense of the contemporary situation. Thus we are treated to self-assertion and self-definition dressed up (in the best fashion) as criticism.

Whether such an analysis—or simply such a feeling—may be taken to be valid or not is finally a matter of faith. It would be my faith, first, that the apocalyptic sensibility represents overwrought reaction to what clearly are a number of cultural crises. Panic is the wrong response to crisis. Second, however desperate one's personalism may have become as an individual, even religious, thing, it is unsuited to teaching. Teaching chaos and old night is antiteaching.

I V

SINCE THIS ALL DOES COME DOWN IN THE END TO MAT-
ters of faith, I must go on and say that I believe that a
work of literature is most importantly an occasion of experience in its reader. Therefore, viable teaching of literature becomes the discovery of ways to make that
experience, or perhaps just more of what is potentially
there, available to students. For the most part, literary
scholarship and criticism perform their real functions as
they enhance teaching. In the context in which we have
been thinking, the key issue becomes the question: shall
the teaching of literature be regarded essentially as an
expressive event or as a *civic* event? Ought teaching literature to be primarily the occasion for unique, personal,
even Dionysian self-revelation? Or ought it to become the
means toward an adventure in community? Should one
respond "creatively" or "responsibly"? And if those
polarities prove not irreconcilable, to what are we ultimately to be responsible? If it be granted that a novel may
indeed stimulate our imaginations to creativity, are
teachers released thereby to become their own bad artists? Or must we work responsibly to be guided to a con-
trolled creativity, to seek intenser, profounder, better
shaped experiences than we could in fact create for ourselves without the novel?

I believe, and passionately, that literary experience
is mainly shared experience, if only because literature
can take subterranean experience and raise it to the common light. It is experience of community, in important
essentials public experience, civil, market-place experience, subject to certain degrees of common investigation
by objective reference to the language of the text and by
sharing insight and response. It is a means of commun-

ion by which one may realize degrees of his oneness with other men, with authors, critics, teachers, and, above all, other readers both near in time or culture and far away.

However exciting or fashionable, the exploitation of authors and their art for the display of personal sensitivities or wishful superiorities, or for a rostrum, or for a smoke screen upon which to project what are, in Norman Mailer's perfect phrase, *Advertisements for Myself,* remains exploitation. It is odious in a critic and immoral in a teacher.

What, on the other hand, are *responsible* criticism and teaching? It is, of course, hard to say in the abstract. But I may suggest some principles. The responsible treatment of literature is *contextual:* it begins with the language of the text and returns to illuminate that language no matter how far afield it has ranged. It is *coherent* in its explanations. It is faithful to the *complete* work, never betraying the work by inventing a false context or taking a part for the whole. It is *comparative,* if need be, to the historical contexts of other writings, the relevant culture or languages; or to the literatures of other places, times, or tongues; or to the "great tradition" of absolute masterpieces. In all these ways it is as faithful to the possibilities of "objectivity"—or at any rate the commonalty of the intellectual market-place—as it is possible for the fickle human mind to be.

INDEX